easy to make!
Chicken

Good Housekeeping

easy to make!
Chicken

COLLINS & BROWN

This edition published in the United Kingdom in 2015
by Collins & Brown
1 Gower Street
London WC1E 6HD

An imprint of Pavilion Books Company Ltd

The Good Housekeeping website is
www.goodhousekeeping.co.uk

10 9 8 7 6 5 4 3 2

ISBN 978-184340-658-7

A catalogue record for this book is available from the British
Library.

Repro by Dot Gradations UK, Ltd
Printed and bound by Times Offset (M) Sdn. Bhd, Malaysia

This book can be ordered direct from the publisher at
www.pavilionbooks.com

Contents

Foreword

Cooking, for me, is one of life's great pleasures. Not only is it necessary to fuel your body, but it exercises creativity, skill, social bonding and patience. The science behind the cooking also fascinates me, learning to understand how yeast works, or to grasp why certain flavours marry quite so well (in my mind) is to become a good cook.

I've often encountered people who claim not to be able to cook – they're just not interested or say they simply don't have time. My sister won't mind me saying that she was one of those who sat firmly in the camp of disinterested domestic goddess. But things change, she realised that my mother (an excellent cook) can't always be on hand to prepare steaming home-cooked meals and that she actually wanted to become a mother one day who was able to whip up good food for her own family. All it took was some good cook books (naturally, Good Housekeeping was present and accounted for) and some enthusiasm and sure enough she is now a kitchen wizard, creating such confections that even baffle me.

I've been lucky enough to have had a love for all things culinary since as long as I can remember. Baking rock-like chocolate cakes and misshapen biscuits was a right of passage that I protectively guard. I made my mistakes young, so have lost the fear of cookery mishaps. I think it's these mishaps that scare people, but when you realise that a mistake made once will seldom be repeated, then kitchen domination can start.

This Good Housekeeping Easy to Make! collection is filled with hundreds of tantalising recipes that have been triple tested (at least!) in our dedicated test kitchens. They have been developed to be easily achievable, delicious and guaranteed to work – taking the chance out of cooking.

I hope you enjoy this collection and that it inspires you to get cooking.

Meike.

Meike Beck
Cookery Director
Good Housekeeping

0

The Basics

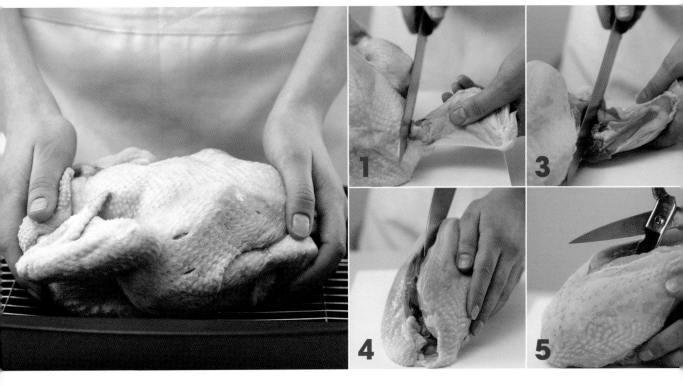

Preparing the bird for cooking

Chicken and other poultry and game birds may be bought whole for roasting or in pieces ready for cooking. It is often cheaper to buy a whole bird, then joint it yourself for cooking as required.

Jointing

1 Using a sharp meat knife with a curved blade, cut out the wishbone, then cut off the wings in a single piece. Remove the wing tips.

2 With the tail pointing towards you and the breast side up, pull one leg away and cut through the skin between the leg and breast. Pull the leg down until you crack the joint between the thigh bone and ribcage.

3 Cut through that joint, then cut through the remaining leg meat. Repeat on the other side.

4 To remove the breast without any bone, make a cut along the length of the breastbone. Gently teasing the flesh away from the ribs with the knife, work the blade down between the flesh and ribs of one breast and cut it off neatly. (Always cut in, towards the bone.) Repeat on the other side.

5 To remove the breast with bone in, make a cut along the full length of the breastbone. Using poultry shears, cut through the breastbone, then cut through the ribcage following the outline of the breast meat. Repeat on the other side. Trim off any flaps of skin or fat.

Trussing

When roasting poultry, it is not necessary to truss it but it gives the bird a neater shape for serving at the table.

1 Cut out the wishbone by pulling back the flap of skin at the neck end and locating the tip of the bone with a small sharp knife. Run the knife along the inside of the bone on both sides, then on the outside. Take care not to cut deep into the breast meat. Use poultry shears or sharp-pointed scissors to snip the tip of the bone from the breastbone, and pull the bone away from the breast. Snip the two ends or pull them out by hand.

2 Pull off any loose fat from the neck or cavity. Put the wing tips under the breast and fold the neck flap on to the back of the bird. Thread a trussing needle and use it to secure the neck flap.

3 Push a metal skewer through both legs, at the joint between thigh and drumstick. Twist some string around both ends of the skewer and pull firmly to tighten.

4 Turn the bird over. Bring the string over the ends of the drumsticks, pull tight and tie to secure the legs.

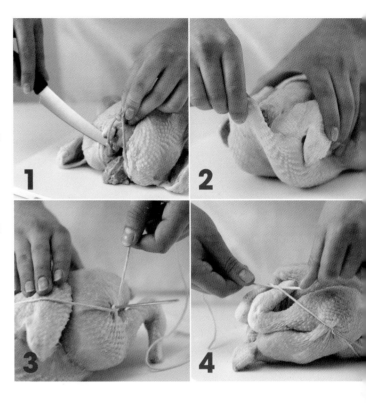

Hygiene

Raw poultry contains harmful bacteria that can spread easily to anything they touch.
Always wash your hands, kitchen surfaces, chopping boards, knives and equipment before and after handling poultry.
Don't let raw poultry touch other foods.
Always cover raw poultry, and store in the bottom of the refrigerator, where it can't touch or drip on to other foods.

Slicing breast fillets

1 Cut or pull out the long strip of flesh lying on the inside of the breast. Slice it across the grain to the thickness required for your recipe. (Raw chicken should not be cut less than about 3mm/$\frac{1}{8}$in thick.)

2 Starting at the small tip of the breast, cut slices of the required thickness. Alternatively, cut into chunks or dice.

Cooking chicken

From simple, healthy stir-frying and steaming to indulgent and flavourful casseroling, there are numerous ways to cook this versatile meat.

Pan-frying

This is a quick method for cooking chicken pieces and you can make a sauce with the pan juices at the end if you like.

1 Put in enough oil (or a mixture of oil and clarified butter) to fill a frying pan to a depth of about 5mm (¼in) and put the pan over a medium heat.

2 Season the chicken with salt and ground black pepper, then carefully add to the pan, flesh side down, and fry for 10–15 minutes until it's browned. (Don't put too many pieces of chicken in the pan at once or the chicken will cook partly in its own steam.)

3 Turn the pieces over and cook on the skin side for another 10–15 minutes until the skin is brown and the flesh is cooked but still juicy all the way through.

4 Remove the chicken from the pan using a pair of tongs and keep warm. Pour off the excess oil and deglaze the pan with a little wine or stock. Stir thoroughly, scraping up the sediment, then add some herbs and finely chopped garlic or onion and cook for a few minutes. Serve the chicken with the sauce.

How to tell if chicken is cooked

Pierce the thickest part of the meat – on a whole roast bird this is usually the thigh – with a skewer. The juices that run out should be golden and clear with no trace of pink; if they're not, return the bird to the oven and check at regular intervals.

Duck and game birds are traditionally served with the meat slightly pink: if overcooked, the meat may be dry.

Marinades

- Marinades will not penetrate poultry skin, so remove the skin or cut slashes in it.
- Use just enough marinade to coat the poultry generously – drowning it is wasteful, as it runs off and most will be left in the bottom of the container.
- To make a simple marinade, combine olive oil, lemon juice and chopped garlic, pour over chicken and marinate in the refrigerator for at least 1 hour.

Grilling

This method is perfect for cooking pieces such as breast fillets or for strips or chunks threaded on to skewers. Small birds can be spatchcocked (the backbone is removed and the bird flattened out) and grilled.

1 Marinate (see opposite) the chicken pieces for 30 minutes, then drain and pat dry. Alternatively, brush the chicken with a flavoured oil. Put the pieces on a wire rack over a grill pan or roasting tin, and set the pan under a preheated grill so that it is about 8cm (3¼in) from the heat source.

2 Every few minutes brush a little of the marinade or a teaspoon of oil over the chicken.

3 When cooked on one side, turn with tongs and cook the other side until cooked through. Avoid piercing the flesh when turning. Allow 12–20 minutes for a breast fillet or kebabs and 20–30 minutes for a spatchcocked bird.

Stir-frying

1 Cut the chicken into small, even-sized strips or dice no more than 5mm (¼in) thick. Heat a wok or large pan until very hot and add oil to coat the inside.

2 Add the chicken and cook, stirring constantly, until just done. Remove to a bowl. Cook the other ingredients you are using for the stir-fry, then return the chicken to the pan and cook for 1–2 minutes to heat through.

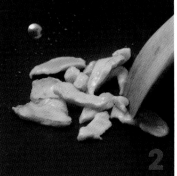

Steaming

1 Cut the chicken into thick shreds or chunks, or use thighs, drumsticks or halved breasts. Marinate (see opposite), if you like, for at least 1 hour.

2 Arrange the chicken in a single layer on a heatproof dish that is small enough to fit inside the steamer. Place in the steamer, cover and steam for 20–40 minutes until just cooked through.

Chicken Casserole

To serve four to six, you will need:
1 chicken, jointed, 3 tbsp olive oil, 1 onion, chopped, 2 garlic cloves, crushed, 2 celery sticks, chopped, 2 carrots, chopped, 1 tbsp plain flour, 2 tbsp chopped tarragon or thyme, chicken stock and/or wine, salt and ground black pepper.

1 Preheat the oven to 180°C (160°C fan oven) mark 4. Cut the chicken legs and breasts in half.

2 Heat the olive oil in a flameproof casserole and brown the chicken all over. Remove and pour off the excess oil. Add the onion and garlic and brown for a few minutes. Add the vegetables, then stir in the flour and cook for 1 minute. Add the herbs and season with salt and pepper. Add the chicken and pour in stock and/or wine to come three-quarters of the way up the chicken pieces. Cook for 1–1½ hours until the chicken is cooked through.

Roasting and carving

A roast chicken has a luxurious aroma and flavour, and it makes an excellent Sunday lunch or special meal with very little preparation. To get the most out of the roast, these few simple guidelines make carving very easy, giving neat slices to serve.

Preparing the bird

1 Take the bird out of the refrigerator 45 minutes–1 hour before roasting to allow it to reach room temperature.

2 Before stuffing a bird for roasting, clean it thoroughly. Put the bird in the sink and pull out and discard any loose fat with your fingers. Then run cold water through the cavity and dry the bird well using kitchen paper.

Roasting times

To calculate the roasting time for a chicken, weigh the oven-ready bird (including stuffing, if using) and allow 20 minutes per 450g (1lb) plus 20 minutes extra. Cook in a preheated oven at 200°C (180°C fan oven) mark 6.

Oven-ready weight (approx.)	Serves	Cooking time
1.4–1.6 kg (3–3½lb)	4–6	1½ hours
1.8–2.3kg (4–5lb)	6–8	1 hour 50 minutes
2.5–2.7kg (5½–6lb)	8–10	2¼ hours

Basting

Chicken, turkey and other poultry needs to be basted regularly during roasting to keep the flesh moist. Use an oven glove to steady the roasting tin and spoon the juices and melted fat over the top of the bird. Alternatively, use a bulb baster.

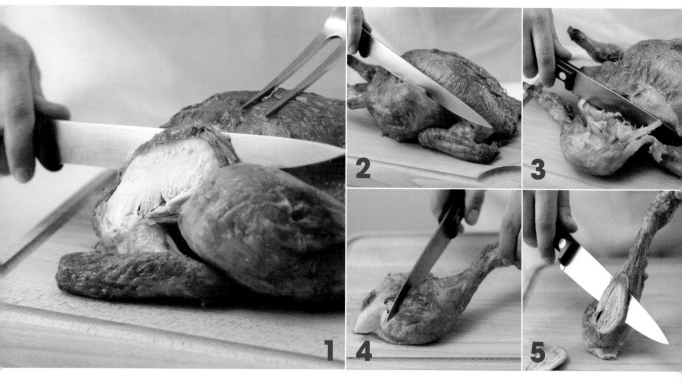

Resting

Once the bird is cooked, allow it to rest before carving. Lift it out of the roasting tin, put it on a plate and cover loosely with foil and a clean teatowel. Resting allows the juices to settle back into the meat, leaving it moist and easier to carve.

Resting times

Grouse and small game birds	10 minutes
Chicken and duck	15 minutes
Turkey and goose	20–30 minutes

Storing leftovers

- -

Don't forget the leftovers when lunch is finished – never leave poultry standing in a warm room. Cool quickly in a cold place, then cover and chill.

Carving chicken

After resting, put the bird on a carving board.

1 Steady the bird with a carving fork. To cut breast meat, start at the neck end and cut slices about 5mm (¼in) thick. Use the carving knife and fork to lift them on to a warmed serving plate.

2 To cut off the legs, cut the skin between the thigh and breast.

3 Pull the leg down to expose the joint between the thigh bone and ribcage, and cut through that joint.

4 Cut through the joint between the thigh and drumstick.

5 To carve meat from the leg (for turkeys and very large chickens), remove it from the carcass and joint the two parts of the leg, as above. Holding the drumstick by the thin end, stand it up on the carving board and carve slices roughly parallel with the bone. The thigh can be carved either flat on the board or upright.

Chicken Stock

For 1.1 litres (2 pints), you will need:
1.6kg (3½lb) chicken bones, 225g (8oz) each onions and celery, sliced, 150g (5oz) leeks, chopped, 1 bouquet garni (2 bay leaves, a few thyme sprigs and a small bunch of parsley), 1 tsp black peppercorns, ½ tsp salt.

1 Put all the ingredients into a large pan and add 3 litres (5¼ pints) cold water. Bring slowly to the boil and skim the surface.

2 Partially cover the pan and simmer gently for 2 hours. Adjust the seasoning if necessary.

3 Strain the stock through a muslin-lined sieve into a bowl and cool quickly. Degrease (see right) before using.

Cook's Tips

- -

Uncooked chicken bones can be used for stock: reserve the bones when you joint a chicken, or ask your butcher to set some bones aside for you. If the chicken has not been previously frozen, the bones can be kept in a sealed plastic bag in the freezer

Alternatively, use the leftover carcass of a roast chicken.

Preparing stock

Good stock can mark the difference between a good dish and a great one. It gives depth of flavour to many dishes and is the perfect base for sauces and soups.

Degreasing stock

Meat and poultry stock needs to be degreased – vegetable stock does not. You can mop the fat from the surface using kitchen paper, but the following methods are easier and more effective. There are three main methods that you can use: ladling, pouring and chilling.

1 **Ladling** While the stock is warm, place a ladle on the surface. Press down and allow the fat floating on the surface to trickle over the edge until the ladle is full. Discard the fat, then repeat until all the fat has been removed.

2 **Pouring** For this you need a degreasing jug or a double-pouring gravy boat, which has the spout at the base of the vessel. When you fill the jug or gravy boat with a fatty liquid, the fat rises. When you pour, the stock comes out while the fat stays behind in the jug.

3 **Chilling** Put the stock in the refrigerator until the fat solidifies, then remove the pieces of fat using a slotted spoon.

Cook's Tips

To get a clearer liquid when making meat or poultry stock, strain the cooked stock through four layers of muslin in a sieve.

Stock will keep for three days in the refrigerator. If you want to keep it for a further three days, transfer it to a pan and reboil gently for 5 minutes. Cool, put into a clean bowl and chill for a further three days.

When making meat or chicken stock, make sure there is a good ratio of meat to bones. The more meat you use, the more flavour the stock will have.

Spring Vegetable Broth

To serve four, you will need:
1 tbsp olive oil, 4 shallots, chopped, 1 fennel bulb, chopped, 1 leek, chopped, 5 small carrots, chopped, 1.1 litres (2 pints) hot fresh chicken stock, 2 courgettes, chopped, 1 bunch asparagus, chopped, 2 x 400g cans cannellini beans, drained and rinsed, 50g (2oz) Gruyère or Parmesan shavings to serve.

1 Heat the olive oil in a large pan. Add the shallots, fennel, leek and carrots, and fry for 5 minutes or until they start to soften.

2 Add the stock, cover and bring to the boil. Add the courgettes, asparagus and beans, then simmer for 5–6 minutes until the vegetables are tender. Ladle into bowls and sprinkle with a little cheese.

Orange, Sage and Thyme Stuffing

To serve eight, you will need:
2 tbsp olive oil, 1 large onion, finely chopped, 2 garlic cloves, crushed, 75g (3oz) fresh white breadcrumbs, 50g (2oz) pinenuts, toasted and chopped, grated zest of 1 orange, plus 2–3 tbsp juice, 2 tbsp each finely chopped fresh thyme and sage, 1 medium egg yolk, beaten, salt and ground black pepper.

1 Heat the olive oil in a pan and fry the onion and garlic gently for 5 minutes until soft but not brown.

2 Put the remaining ingredients in a large bowl. Add the onion mixture and stir to bind, adding more orange juice if needed.

Bacon, Pecan and Wild Rice Stuffing

To serve eight, you will need:
900ml (1½ pints) hot chicken stock, 1 bay leaf, 1 thyme sprig, 225g (8oz) mixed long-grain and wild rice, 50g (2oz) unsalted butter, 225g (8oz) smoked streaky bacon, roughly chopped, 2 onions, finely chopped, 3 celery sticks, finely chopped, ½ Savoy cabbage, chopped, 3 tbsp finely chopped marjoram, 85g sachet sage and onion stuffing mix, 125g (4oz) pecans, chopped.

1 Put the chicken stock in a pan, add the bay leaf and thyme and bring to the boil. Add the rice, cover, reduce the heat and cook according to the pack instructions. Drain if necessary, then tip into a large bowl and cool quickly, discarding the herbs.

2 Melt the butter in a large pan, add the bacon, onions and celery, and cook over a medium heat for 10 minutes until the onions are soft but not brown. Add the cabbage and marjoram and cook for 5 minutes, stirring regularly.

3 Add the cabbage mixture to the rice, together with the stuffing mix and pecans. Tip into a bowl and cool quickly.

Stuffings

These stuffings are suitable for chicken, turkey or goose. All can be made a day ahead and chilled overnight. Alternatively – with the exception of the wild rice stuffing – all can be frozen for up to one month. Thaw overnight in the refrigerator before using to stuff the bird.

Falafel Balls

These stuffing balls are delicious with chicken, but are also great with pitta bread and salad as a vegetarian meal.

To serve eight to ten, you will need:
275g (10oz) dried chickpeas, 1 small onion, roughly chopped, 1 small handful of fresh coriander, 3 garlic cloves, roughly chopped, juice of 1/2 lemon, 2 tsp ground cumin, 1/2 tsp bicarbonate of soda, olive oil for shallow-frying, salt and ground black pepper.

1 Put the chickpeas in a pan and cover with plenty of cold water. Bring to the boil and boil for 2 minutes, then leave to soak for 2 hours. Drain.

2 Put the drained chickpeas into a food processor with the onion, coriander, garlic, lemon juice, cumin, bicarbonate of soda and 1/2 tsp salt and pepper. Whiz until everything is finely ground and beginning to stick together. Take small handfuls of the mixture and squeeze in the palm of your hand to extract any excess moisture. Shape into walnut-sized balls.

3 Heat the olive oil in a frying pan over a medium-high heat and fry the falafel for 3–4 minutes until they are deep golden brown all over. Drain well on kitchen paper. Serve immediately, or chill for later use.

4 To use, put the falafel in a parcel of foil and reheat alongside the roast for 15–20 minutes.

Rosemary and Lemon Stuffing

To serve four to six, you will need:
25g (1oz) butter, 1 onion, finely chopped, 125g (4oz) fresh white breadcrumbs, 1 tbsp freshly chopped rosemary leaves, grated zest of 1 lemon, 1 medium egg, beaten, salt and ground black pepper.

1 Melt the butter in a pan, then fry the onion over a low heat for 10–15 minutes until soft and golden. Tip into a bowl and cool.

2 Add the breadcrumbs, rosemary leaves and lemon zest. Season well, then add the egg and stir to bind.

Pork, Chestnut and Orange Stuffing

To serve eight to ten, you will need:
50g (2oz) butter, 6 shallots, roughly chopped, 4 celery sticks, roughly chopped, 1 fresh rosemary sprig, snipped, 1 tbsp chopped flat-leafed parsley, 175g (6oz) firm white bread, cut into rough dice, 2 cooking apples, about 225g (8oz) total weight, peeled, cored and chopped, 125g (4oz) cooked, peeled (or vacuum-packed) chestnuts, roughly chopped, grated zest of 1 large orange, 450g (1lb) coarse pork sausagemeat, salt and ground black pepper.

1 Melt the butter in a large frying pan and gently fry the shallots, celery and rosemary for 10–12 minutes until the vegetables are soft and golden. Tip into a large bowl. Add the parsley, bread, apples, chestnuts and orange zest to the bowl. Season and mix well.

2 Divide the sausagemeat into walnut-sized pieces. Fry, in batches, until golden and cooked through. Add to the bowl and stir to mix.

Pork, Spinach and Apple Stuffing

To serve eight, you will need:
2 tbsp olive oil, 150g (5oz) onion, finely chopped, 225g (8oz) fresh spinach, torn into pieces if the leaves are large, 2 sharp apples, such as Granny Smith, peeled, cored and cut into chunks, 400g (14oz) pork sausagemeat, coarsely grated zest of 1 lemon, 1 tbsp chopped thyme, 100g (3 1/2oz) fresh white breadcrumbs, 2 large eggs, beaten, salt and ground black pepper.

1 Heat the olive oil in a frying pan, add the onion and cook for 10 minutes or until soft. Increase the heat, add the spinach and cook until wilted.

2 Add the apples and cook, stirring, for 2–3 minutes, then set aside to cool. When the mixture is cold, add the sausagemeat, lemon zest, thyme, breadcrumbs and eggs, then season and stir until evenly mixed.

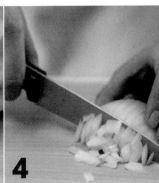

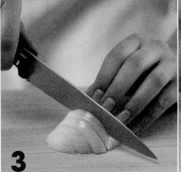

Onions

1 Cut off the tip and base of the onion. Peel away all the layers of papery skin and any discoloured layers underneath.

2 Put the onion root end down on the chopping board, then, using a sharp knife, cut the onion in half from tip to base.

3 **Slicing** Put one half on the board with the cut surface facing down and slice across the onion.

4 **Chopping** Slice the halved onions from the root end to the top at regular intervals. Next, make 2–3 horizontal slices through the onion, then slice vertically across the width.

Preparing vegetables

Nutritious, mouthwatering and essential to a healthy diet – vegetables are a must in every kitchen. Not all vegetables need to be peeled. Some vegetables become discoloured after peeling, and need to be placed in acidulated water (water and lemon juice) to slow the discolouration down – the recipe will tell you when this is necessary.

Shallots

1 Cut off the tip and trim off the ends of the root. Peel off the skin and any discoloured layers underneath.

2 Holding the shallot with the root end down, use a small, sharp knife to make deep parallel slices almost down to the base while keeping the slices attached to it.

3 **Slicing** Turn the shallot on its side and cut off slices from the base.

4 **Dicing** Make deep parallel slices at right angles to the first slices. Turn the shallot on its side and cut off the slices from the base. You should now have fine dice, but chop any larger pieces individually.

Peeling tomatoes

1 Fill a bowl or pan with boiling water. Using a slotted spoon, add the tomato for 15–30 seconds, then remove to a chopping board.

2 Use a small sharp knife to cut out the core in a single cone-shaped piece. Discard the core.

3 Peel off the skin; it should come away easily depending on ripeness.

Seeding unpeeled tomatoes

1 Halve the tomato through the core. Use a small sharp knife or a teaspoon to remove the seeds and juice. Shake off the excess liquid.

2 Chop the tomato as required for your recipe and place in a colander for a minute or two, to drain off any excess liquid.

Peppers

Red, green and yellow peppers all contain seeds and white pith which taste bitter and should be removed.
Cut the pepper in half vertically, discard the seeds and core, then trim away the rest of the white membrane with a small sharp knife. Alternatively, slice the top off the pepper, then cut away and discard the seeds and pith. Cut the pepper into strips or slices.

Fennel

1 Trim off the top stems and the base of the bulbs. Remove the core with a small sharp knife if it is tough.

2 The outer leaves may be discoloured and can be scrubbed gently in cold water, or you can peel away the discoloured parts with a knife or a vegetable peeler. Slice or chop the fennel.

Celery

To remove the strings in the outer green stalks, trim the ends and cut into the base of the stalk with a small knife; catch the strings between the blade and your thumb. Pull up towards the top of the stalk to remove the string.

Mushrooms

Button, white, chestnut and flat mushrooms are all prepared in a similar way.
Shiitake mushrooms have a hard stalk; cut it off and use for making stock if you like.

1 Wipe with a damp cloth or pastry brush to remove any dirt.

2 With button mushrooms, cut off the stalk flush with the base of the cap. For other mushrooms, cut a thin disc off the end of the stalk and discard. Quarter or slice as needed.

Leeks

As some leeks harbour a lot of grit and earth between their leaves, they need careful cleaning.

1 Cut off the root and any tough parts of the leek. Make a cut into the leaf end of the leek, about 7.5cm (3in) deep.

2 Hold under the cold tap while separating the cut halves to expose any grit. Wash well, then shake dry. Slice, cut into matchsticks or slice diagonally.

1

Flavourings

Flavourings make the difference between a good dish and a really delicious one. Many chicken stir-fry recipes begin by cooking garlic, ginger and spring onions as the basic flavourings. Spicier dishes may include chillies, lemongrass or a prepared spice paste such as Thai curry paste.

Ginger

1 **Grating** Cut off a piece of the root and peel with a vegetable peeler. Cut off any brown spots.

2 Rest the grater on a board or small plate and grate the ginger. Discard any large fibres adhering to the pulp.

3 **Slicing, shredding and chopping** Cut slices off the ginger and cut off the skin carefully. Cut off any brown spots. Stack the slices and cut into shreds. To chop, stack the shreds and cut across into small pieces.

4 **Pressing** If you just need the ginger juice, peel and cut off any brown spots, then cut into small chunks and use a garlic press held over a small bowl to extract the juice.

Spring onions

Cut off the roots and trim any coarse or withered green parts. Slice diagonally, chop finely, or shred by cutting into 5cm (2in) lengths then slicing down the lengths, according to the recipe.

Lemongrass

Lemongrass is a popular South-east Asian ingredient, giving an aromatic lemony flavour. It looks rather like a long, slender spring onion, but is fibrous and woody and is usually removed before the dish is served. Alternatively the inner leaves may be very finely chopped or pounded in a mortar and pestle and used in spice pastes.

Garlic

1 Put the clove on a chopping board and place the flat side of a large knife on top of it. Press down firmly on the flat of the blade to crush the clove and break the papery skin.

2 Cut off the base of the clove and slip the garlic out of its skin. It should come away easily.

3 **Slicing** Using a rocking motion with the knife tip on the board, slice the garlic as thinly as you need.

4 **Shredding and chopping** Holding the slices together, shred them across the slices. Chop the shreds if you need chopped garlic.

5 **Crushing** After step 2, the whole clove can be put into a garlic press. Alternatively, to crush with a knife: roughly chop the peeled cloves with a pinch of salt. Press down hard with the edge of a large knife tip (with the blade facing away from you), then drag the blade along the garlic while still pressing hard. Continue to do this, dragging the knife over the garlic.

Chillies

1 Cut off the cap and slit open lengthways. Using a teaspoon, scrape out the seeds and the pith.

2 **Dicing** Cut into thin shreds lengthways, then cut crossways.

Cook's Tip

Chillies vary enormously in strength, from quite mild to blisteringly hot, depending on the type of chilli and its ripeness. Taste a small piece first to check it's not too hot for you. **Be extremely careful** when handling chillies not to touch or rub your eyes with your fingers, or they will sting. Wash knives immediately after handling chillies. As a precaution, use rubber gloves when preparing them, if you like.

Asian flavourings and ingredients

The following items, used in many Asian dishes, are available in large supermarkets and Asian food shops.

Spices

Chinese five-spice powder is made from star anise, fennel seeds, cinnamon, cloves and Sichuan pepper. It has a strong liquorice-like flavour and should be used sparingly.

Kaffir lime leaves, used in South-east Asian cooking for their lime-lemon flavour, are glossy leaves used whole but not eaten – rather like bay leaves. Use grated lime zest as a substitute.

Tamarind paste has a delicately sour flavour; use lemon juice as a substitute.

Sauces

Soy sauce – made from fermented soya beans and, usually, wheat – is the most common flavouring in Chinese and South-east Asian cooking. There are light and dark soy sauces; the dark kind is slightly sweeter and tends to darken the food. It will keep indefinitely.

Thai fish sauce is a salty condiment with a distinctive, pungent aroma. It is used in many South-east Asian dishes. It will keep indefinitely.

Thai green curry paste is a blend of spices such as green chillies, coriander and lemongrass. Once opened, store in a sealed container in the refrigerator for up to one month.

Thai red curry paste contains fresh and dried red chillies and ginger. Once opened, store in a sealed container in the refrigerator for up to one month.

Chilli sauce is made from fresh red chillies, vinegar, salt and sugar; some versions include other ingredients such as garlic or ginger. Sweet chilli sauce is a useful standby for adding piquancy to all kinds of dishes.

Black bean sauce is made from fermented black beans, salt and ginger. Salty and pungent on its own, it adds richness to many stir-fry dishes.

Yellow bean sauce is a thick, salty, aromatic yellow-brown purée of fermented yellow soya beans, flour and salt.

Hoisin sauce, sometimes called barbecue sauce, is a thick, sweet-spicy red-brown sauce.

Oyster sauce is a smooth brown sauce made from oyster extract, wheat flour and other flavourings. It doesn't taste fishy, but adds a 'meaty' flavour to stir-fries and braises.

Plum sauce, made from plums, ginger, chillies, vinegar and sugar, is traditionally served with duck or as a dip.

Canned vegetables

Bamboo shoots, available sliced or in chunks, have a mild flavour; rinse before use.

Water chestnuts have a very mild flavour but add a lovely crunch to stir-fried and braised dishes.

Other ingredients

Dried mushrooms feature in some Chinese recipes; they need to be soaked in hot water for 30 minutes before use.

Dried shrimps and dried shrimp paste (blachan) are often used in South-east Asian cooking. The pungent smell becomes milder during cooking and marries with the other ingredients. These are often included in ready-made sauces and spice pastes, and are not suitable for vegetarians.

Mirin is a sweet rice wine from Japan; if you can't find it, use dry or medium sherry instead.

Rice wine is often used in Chinese cooking; if you can't find it, use dry sherry instead.

Rice vinegar is clear and milder than other vinegars. Use white wine vinegar or cider vinegar as a substitute.

Using herbs

Most herbs are the leaf of a flowering plant, and are usually sold with much of the stalk intact. They have to be washed, trimmed and then chopped or torn into pieces suitable for your recipe.

Washing

1 Trim the roots and part of the stalks from the herbs. Immerse the herbs in cold water and shake briskly. Leave in the water for a few minutes.

2 Lift out of the water and put in a colander or sieve, then rinse again under the cold tap. Leave to drain for a few minutes, then dry thoroughly on kitchen paper or teatowels, or use a salad spinner.

Chopping

1 Trim the herbs by pinching off all but the smallest, most tender stalks. If the herb is one with a woody stalk, such as rosemary or thyme, it may be easier to remove the leaves by rubbing the whole bunch between your hands; the leaves should simply pull off the stems.

2 If you are chopping the leaves, gather them into a compact ball in one hand, keeping your fist around the ball (but being careful not to crush them).

3 Chop with a large knife, using a rocking motion and letting just a little of the ball out of your fingers at a time.

4 When the herbs are roughly chopped, continue chopping until the pieces are in small shreds or flakes.

Citrus fruits

Citrus zest is an important flavouring and is simple to prepare. Segments or slices of citrus used in recipes need to be prepared so that no skin, pith or membrane remains.

Zesting

1 Wash and thoroughly dry the fruit. Using a zester, grater or vegetable peeler, cut away the zest (the coloured outer layer of skin), taking care to leave behind the bitter white pith. Continue until you have removed as much as you need.

2 Stack the slices of zest on a board and, using a sharp knife, shred or dice as required.

Segmenting

1 Cut off a slice at both ends of the fruit, then cut off the peel, just inside the white pith.

2 Hold the fruit over a bowl to catch the juice and cut between the segments just inside the membrane to release the flesh. Continue until all the segments are removed. Squeeze the juice from the membrane into the bowl and use as required.

Perfect herbs

- Don't pour the herbs and their water into the sieve, because dirt in the water might get caught in the leaves.
- If the herb has fleshy stalks, such as parsley or coriander, the stalks can be saved to flavour stock or soup. Tie them in a bundle with string for easy removal.

Cooking rice, grains and potatoes

Wholesome and healthy, rice, grains and potatoes can be nutritious everyday staples. Easy to prepare and cook, they are also very economical and they store well.

Cooking rice

There are two main types of rice: long-grain and short-grain. Long-grain rice is generally served as an accompaniment; the most commonly used type of long-grain rice in South-east Asian cooking is jasmine rice, also known as Thai fragrant rice. It has a distinctive taste and slightly sticky texture. Long-grain rice needs no special preparation, although it should be washed to remove excess starch. Put the rice in a bowl and cover with cold water. Stir until this becomes cloudy, then drain and repeat until the water is clear.

Long-grain rice

1 Use 50–75g (2–3oz) raw rice per person; measured by volume 50–75ml (2–2½fl oz). Measure the rice by volume and put it in a pan with a pinch of salt and twice the volume of boiling water (or stock).

2 Bring to the boil. Turn the heat down to low and set the timer for the time stated on the pack. The rice should be al dente: tender with a bite at the centre.

3 When the rice is cooked, fluff up the grains with a fork.

Perfect rice

Use 50–75g (2–3oz) raw rice per person – or measure by volume 50–75ml (2–2½fl oz).
If you cook rice often, you may want to invest in a special rice steamer. They are available in Asian supermarkets and some kitchen shops and give good, consistent results.

Couscous

Often mistaken for a grain, couscous is actually a type of pasta that originated in North Africa. It is perfect for making into salads or serving with stews and casseroles. The tiny pellets do not require cooking and can simply be soaked.

1 Measure the couscous in a jug and add 1½ times the volume of hot water or stock.

2 Cover the bowl and leave to soak for 5 minutes. Fluff up with a fork before serving.

3 If using for a salad, leave the couscous to cool completely before adding the other salad ingredients.

Bulgur wheat

A form of cracked wheat, bulgur has had some or all of the bran removed. It is good used in salads or served as a grain. It is pre-boiled during manufacturing and may be boiled, steamed or soaked.

Simmering Place the bulgur in a pan and cover with water by about 2.5cm (1in). Bring to the boil, then simmer for 10–15 minutes until just tender. Drain well.

Steaming Line a steamer with a clean teatowel, place the bulgur in the steamer and steam over boiling water for 20 minutes or until the grains are soft.

Soaking Put the bulgur in a deep bowl. Cover with hot water and mix with a fork. Leave to steep for 20 minutes, checking to make sure there is enough water. Drain and fluff up with a fork.

Boiling potatoes

1 Peel or scrub old potatoes, scrape or scrub new potatoes. Cut large potatoes into even-sized chunks and put them in a pan with plenty of salted cold water.

2 Cover, bring to the boil, then reduce the heat and simmer until tender – about 10 minutes for new potatoes, 15–20 minutes for old.

Mashing potatoes

To serve four, you will need:
900g (2lb) floury potatoes such as Maris Piper, 125ml (4fl oz) full-fat milk, 25g (1oz) butter, salt and ground black pepper.

1 Peel the potatoes and cut into even-sized chunks. Boil as above until just tender, 15–20 minutes. Test with a small knife. Drain well.

2 Put the potatoes back in the pan and cover with a clean teatowel for 5 minutes, or warm them over a very low heat until the moisture has evaporated.

3 Pour the milk into a small pan and bring to the boil. Pour on to the potatoes with the butter and season with salt and pepper.

4 Mash the potatoes until smooth.

Food storage and hygiene

Storing food properly and preparing it in a hygienic way is important to ensure that food remains as nutritious and flavourful as possible, and to reduce the risk of food poisoning.

Hygiene

When you are preparing food, always follow these important guidelines:

Wash your hands thoroughly before handling food and again between handling different types of food, such as raw and cooked meat and poultry. If you have any cuts or grazes on your hands, be sure to keep them covered with a waterproof plaster.

Wash down worksurfaces regularly with a mild detergent solution or multi-surface cleaner.

Use a dishwasher if available. Otherwise, wear rubber gloves for washing-up, so that the water temperature can be hotter than unprotected hands can bear. Change drying-up cloths and cleaning cloths regularly. Note that leaving dishes to drain is more hygienic than drying them with a teatowel.

Keep raw and cooked foods separate, especially meat, fish and poultry. Wash kitchen utensils in between preparing raw and cooked foods. Never put cooked or ready-to-eat foods directly on to a surface which has just had raw fish, meat or poultry on it.

Keep pets out of the kitchen if possible; or make sure they stay away from worksurfaces. Never allow animals on to worksurfaces.

Shopping

Always choose fresh ingredients in prime condition from stores and markets that have a regular turnover of stock to ensure you buy the freshest produce possible.

Make sure items are within their 'best before' or 'use by' date. (Foods with a longer shelf life have a 'best before' date; more perishable items have a 'use by' date.)

Pack frozen and chilled items in an insulated cool bag at the check-out and put them into the freezer or refrigerator as soon as you get home.

During warm weather in particular, buy perishable foods just before you return home. When packing items at the check-out, sort them according to where you will store them when you get home – the refrigerator, freezer, storecupboard, vegetable rack, fruit bowl, etc. This will make unpacking easier – and quicker.

The storecupboard

Although storecupboard ingredients will generally last a long time, correct storage is important:

Always check packaging for storage advice – even with familiar foods, because storage requirements may change if additives, sugar or salt have been reduced.

Check storecupboard foods for their 'best before' or 'use by' date and do not use them if the date has passed.

Keep all food cupboards scrupulously clean and make sure food containers and packets are properly sealed.

Once opened, treat canned foods as though fresh. Always transfer the contents to a clean container, cover and keep in the refrigerator. Similarly, jars, sauce bottles and cartons should be kept chilled after opening. (Check the label for safe storage times after opening.)

Transfer dry goods such as sugar, rice and pasta to moisture-proof containers. When supplies are used up, wash the container well and thoroughly dry before refilling with new supplies.

Store oils in a dark cupboard away from any heat source as heat and light can make them turn rancid and affect their colour. For the same reason, buy olive oil in dark green bottles.

Store vinegars in a cool place; they can turn bad in a warm environment.

Store dried herbs, spices and flavourings in a cool, dark cupboard or in dark jars. Buy in small quantities as their flavour will not last indefinitely.

Refrigerator storage

Fresh food needs to be kept in the cool temperature of the refrigerator to keep it in good condition and discourage the growth of harmful bacteria. Store day-to-day perishable items, such as opened jams and jellies, mayonnaise and bottled sauces, in the refrigerator along with eggs and dairy products, fruit juices, bacon, fresh and cooked meat (on separate shelves), and salads and vegetables (except potatoes, which don't suit being stored in the cold). A refrigerator should be kept at an operating temperature of 4–5°C. It is worth investing in a refrigerator thermometer to ensure the correct temperature is maintained.

To ensure your refrigerator is functioning effectively for safe food storage, follow these guidelines:

To avoid bacterial cross-contamination, store cooked and raw foods on separate shelves, putting cooked foods on the top shelf. Ensure that all items are well wrapped.

Never put hot food into the refrigerator, as this will cause the internal temperature of the refrigerator to rise.

Avoid overfilling the refrigerator, as this restricts the circulation of air and prevents the appliance from working properly.

It can take some time for the refrigerator to return to the correct operating temperature once the door has been opened, so don't leave it open any longer than is necessary.

Clean the refrigerator regularly, using a specially formulated germicidal refrigerator cleaner. Alternatively, use a weak solution of bicarbonate of soda: 1 tbsp to 1 litre (1¾ pints) water.

If your refrigerator doesn't have an automatic defrost facility, defrost regularly.

Maximum refrigerator storage times

For pre-packed foods, always adhere to the 'use by' date on the pack. For other foods the following storage times should apply, providing the food is in prime condition when it goes into the refrigerator and that your refrigerator is in good working order:

Raw Meat

Bacon	7 days
Game	2 days
Minced meat	1 day
Offal	1 day
Poultry	2 days
Raw sliced meat	2 days

Cooked Meat

Sliced meat	2 days
Ham	2 days
Ham, vacuum-packed (or according to the instructions on the pack)	1–2 weeks

Vegetables

Green vegetables	3–4 days
Salad leaves	2–3 days

Dairy Food

Eggs	1 week
Milk	4–5 days

Fish

Fish	1 day
Shellfish	1 day

Light Bites and Snacks

Easy Wrap

1 tsp salt

1 tsp pepper

2 cooked chicken breasts, about 125g (4oz) each, cut into bite-size pieces

1 carrot, grated

1 avocado, chopped

small handful of rocket

juice of ½ lemon

3 tbsp mayonnaise

4 flour tortillas

1 Mix the salt with the pepper in a large bowl. Add the chicken, carrot, avocado and rocket and mix well.

2 In a separate bowl, mix the lemon juice with the mayonnaise, then spread over the tortillas. Divide the chicken mixture among the tortillas, roll up and serve in napkins, if you like.

Serves	EASY		NUTRITIONAL INFORMATION	
4	**Preparation Time** 10 minutes		**Per Serving** 269 calories, 16g fat (of which 3g saturates), 17g carbohydrate, 1.7g salt	Dairy free

Try Something Different

Use mini poppadoms instead of croustades.
Replace the chutney with cranberry sauce.
Instead of roast chicken, use turkey.

Tangy Chicken Bites

2 x 50g packs mini croustades

about 275g (10oz) fruity chutney, such as mango

2 ready-roasted chicken breasts, skinned, about 125g (4oz) each, torn into small pieces

250g carton crème fraîche

a few fresh thyme sprigs

1 Put the croustades on a board. Spoon about ½ tsp chutney into each one.

2 Top with a few shreds of chicken, a small dollop of crème fraîche and a few thyme leaves. Transfer the croustades to a large serving plate and serve immediately.

EASY		NUTRITIONAL INFORMATION	**Makes**
Preparation Time 10 minutes		**Per Bite** 43 calories, 2g fat (of which 1g saturates), 4g carbohydrate, 0.1g salt	**48**

Chunky Pâté with Port and Green Peppercorns

350g (12oz) boneless belly pork, rind removed, roughly chopped

1 large skinless chicken breast, about 150g (5oz)

225g (8oz) chicken livers, trimmed

1 large duck breast, about 200g (7oz), skinned and chopped into small pieces

125g (4oz) rindless streaky bacon rashers, diced

3 tbsp port or brandy

1 tbsp freshly chopped rosemary

2 tbsp green peppercorns

salt and ground black pepper

crusty bread to serve

To finish

a few bay leaves

2 tsp powdered gelatine

150ml (¼ pint) white port or sherry

1 Preheat the oven to 170°C (150°C fan oven) mark 3. Coarsely mince the belly pork in a food processor, retaining some small chunks. Mince the chicken breast in the processor, then mince the chicken livers.

2 Mix all the meats together in a large bowl with the port or brandy, 1 tsp salt, some pepper, the chopped rosemary and green peppercorns.

3 Pack the mixture into a 1.1 litre (2 pint) terrine and stand in a roasting tin containing 2.5cm (1in) boiling water. Cover with foil and cook in the oven for 1 hour.

4 Remove the foil and arrange a few bay leaves on top of the pâté. Cook for a further 30 minutes or until the juices run clear when the pâté is pierced in the centre with a skewer.

5 Drain the meat juices into a small bowl and leave to cool. Skim off any fat, then sprinkle over the gelatine and leave until softened. Stand the bowl in a pan of gently simmering water until the gelatine has dissolved. Stir in the port or sherry. Make up to 450ml (¾ pint) with water, if necessary.

6 Pour the jellied liquid over the pâté and chill until set. Store the pâté in the refrigerator for up to two days. Serve with crusty bread.

A LITTLE EFFORT		NUTRITIONAL INFORMATION		Serves
Preparation Time 25 minutes, plus setting	**Cooking Time** about 1½ hours	**Per Serving** 344 calories, 22g fat (of which 8g saturates), 3g carbohydrate, 0.7g salt	Dairy free	**8**

Cook's Tip

Bird's eye chillies are hot, so use less for a milder flavour.

1 tbsp each coriander seeds and cumin seeds

2 tsp ground turmeric

4 garlic cloves, roughly chopped

grated zest and juice of 1 lemon

2 bird's eye chillies, seeded and finely chopped (see page 23)

3 tbsp vegetable oil

4 skinless chicken breasts, about 550g (1¼ lb) total weight, cut into finger-length strips

salt and ground black pepper

½ cucumber, cut into sticks, to serve

For the satay sauce

200g (7oz) salted peanuts

1 tbsp molasses sugar

½ lemongrass stalk, chopped

2 tbsp dark soy sauce

juice of ½ lime

200ml (7fl oz) coconut cream

Chicken Satay Skewers

1 Put the coriander and cumin seeds and the turmeric into a dry frying pan and heat for 30 seconds. Tip into a blender and add the garlic, lemon zest and juice, chillies, 1 tbsp vegetable oil and 1 tsp salt. Whiz for 1–2 minutes until smooth.

2 Put the paste into a large, shallow dish, add the chicken and toss everything together. Cover and chill for at least 20 minutes or up to 12 hours.

3 Put all the satay sauce ingredients into a processor and add 2 tbsp water. Whiz to make a thick, chunky sauce, then spoon into a dish. Cover and chill.

4 Preheat the barbecue or grill until hot. Soak 24 wooden skewers in water for 20 minutes. Thread the chicken on to the skewers, drizzle with the remaining oil and grill for 4–5 minutes on each side until the juices run clear when the chicken is pierced with a skewer. Serve with the satay sauce and the cucumber sticks.

Serves	EASY		NUTRITIONAL INFORMATION	
4	**Preparation Time** 30 minutes, plus at least 20 minutes chilling	**Cooking Time** 5 minutes	**Per Serving** 687 calories, 51g fat (of which 21g saturates), 11g carbohydrate, 2.1g salt	Dairy free

Cook's Tip

For a lower-fat version, bake the goujons in the oven. Preheat the oven to 200°C (180°C fan oven) mark 6. Put the goujons on a lightly oiled baking sheet, brush each with a little oil and bake for 12–15 minutes until golden and cooked through.

Lime and Chilli Chicken Goujons

300g (11oz) boneless, skinless chicken thighs

50g (2oz) fresh breadcrumbs

50g (2oz) plain flour

2 tsp dried chilli flakes

grated zest of 1 lime

1 medium egg, beaten

2 tbsp sunflower oil

salt and ground black pepper

lime wedges to serve

For the dip

6 tbsp natural yogurt

6 tbsp mayonnaise

¼ cucumber, halved, deseeded and finely diced

25g (1oz) fresh coriander, chopped

juice of 1 lime

1 Put all the dip ingredients into a bowl. Season with salt and pepper and mix well, then chill.

2 Cut the chicken into strips. Put the breadcrumbs into a bowl with the flour, chilli flakes, lime zest and 1 tsp salt. Mix well. Pour the egg on to a plate. Dip the chicken strips in egg, then coat in the breadcrumb mixture.

3 Heat the oil in a frying pan over a medium heat. Fry the chicken in batches for 7–10 minutes until golden and cooked through. Keep warm while cooking the remainder. Transfer to a serving plate, sprinkle with a little salt, then serve with the dip and lime wedges.

EASY		NUTRITIONAL INFORMATION	Serves
Preparation Time 15 minutes	**Cooking Time** 20 minutes	**Per Serving** 339 calories, 22g fat (of which 4g saturates), 22g carbohydrate, 1.9g salt	**4**

Chicken Falafels

450g (1lb) minced chicken

3 shallots, finely chopped

125g (4oz) canned chickpeas (about ½ can), drained and rinsed

2.5cm (1in) piece fresh root ginger, grated

½ tsp salt

20g (¾oz) fresh coriander, chopped

1 medium egg

3 tbsp olive oil

400g can chopped tomatoes

1 tsp caster sugar

For the couscous salad

200g (7oz) couscous

350ml (12fl oz) hot chicken stock

grated zest and juice of ½ lemon

25g (1oz) pinenuts

seeds from ½ pomegranate

3 tbsp extra virgin olive oil

2–3 tbsp freshly chopped parsley

1 First, make the couscous salad, put the couscous in a bowl and add the hot stock and lemon zest. Leave to soak for 20 minutes. Meanwhile, toast the pinenuts in a pan until golden. Use a fork to fluff up the couscous, then stir in the pinenuts, pomegranate seeds, lemon juice, olive oil and parsley.

2 Put the chicken mince into a food processor. Add 1 chopped shallot, the chickpeas, grated ginger and salt. Whiz to combine.

3 Add the coriander and egg, and whiz again briefly. With damp hands, shape into 12 balls, each measuring 6.5cm (2½in).

4 Heat 2 tbsp olive oil in a frying pan. Fry the patties for 2–3 minutes on each side until golden brown.

5 Meanwhile, fry the remaining shallots in a pan with the remaining oil. Stir in the tomatoes and sugar. Simmer for 10 minutes or until slightly thickened. Serve the patties with the couscous salad, with the sauce on the side.

Serves 4	EASY		NUTRITIONAL INFORMATION	
	Preparation Time 20 minutes	**Cooking Time** 20 minutes	**Per Serving** 287 calories, 14g fat (of which 3g saturates), 10g carbohydrate, 1.1g salt	Dairy free

Chicken Enchiladas

450g (1lb) skinless chicken breasts, cut into strips

1 tsp dried oregano

1 tsp cumin seeds

5 tbsp olive oil, plus extra to grease

2 onions, finely chopped

125g (4oz) celery, cut into strips

2 garlic cloves, crushed

50g (2oz) sun-dried tomatoes in oil, drained and roughly chopped

225g (8oz) brown-cap mushrooms, chopped

250g (9oz) Cheddar cheese, grated

2 tbsp freshly chopped coriander

2 tbsp lemon juice

6 flour tortillas

salt and ground black pepper

salsa verde to serve (see page 41)

1 Preheat the oven to 180°C (160°C fan oven) mark 4. Put the chicken into a bowl, add the oregano, cumin seeds, salt and pepper and toss to coat the chicken.

2 Heat half the olive oil in a large frying pan. Add the onions, celery and garlic. Cook gently for 5–7 minutes. Add the tomatoes and mushrooms, and cook for 2–3 minutes. Remove from the pan and set aside.

3 Add the remaining oil to the pan and stir-fry the chicken in batches for 2–3 minutes. Add the chicken to the mushroom mixture, with 175g (6oz) cheese, the chopped coriander and lemon juice. Mix well and season with salt and pepper to taste.

4 Divide the chicken mixture among the tortillas and roll up to enclose the filling. Put, seam-side down, into an oiled ovenproof dish, then sprinkle with the remaining cheese. Cook in the oven for 25–30 minutes until golden and bubbling. Spoon the salsa verde over the enchiladas to serve.

Serves	EASY		NUTRITIONAL INFORMATION
6	**Preparation Time** 30 minutes	**Cooking Time** 50 minutes	**Per Serving** 433 calories, 17g fat (of which 10g saturates), 37g carbohydrate, 1.3g salt

50g (2oz) walnuts

1 loaf walnut bread, cut into 1cm (½in) slices

2 tbsp olive oil

1 tbsp sea salt flakes

175g (6oz) cooked chicken breast, cut into 15 slices

125g (4oz) sun-dried tomatoes in oil, drained and sliced into 15 pieces

freshly chopped flat-leafed parsley to garnish

For the salsa verde

3 tbsp each roughly chopped fresh coriander, mint and basil

1 garlic clove, roughly chopped

2 tbsp Dijon mustard

3 anchovy fillets

1 tbsp capers

50ml (2fl oz) olive oil

juice of ½ lemon

Chicken and Salsa Verde Crostini

1 Put the walnuts into a dry pan and toast over a medium-high heat, tossing regularly, for 2–3 minutes or until golden brown. Chop finely and set aside.

2 Put all the salsa verde ingredients into a food processor or blender and whiz until smooth. (Alternatively, use a mortar and pestle.) Cover and chill.

3 Preheat the grill to high. Cut the bread slices into 2.5cm (1in) pieces. Put on a baking sheet, brush with olive oil and sprinkle with sea salt flakes. Grill for 1 minute on each side or until lightly toasted.

4 To serve, put a slice of chicken on each crostini base, top with a spoonful of salsa verde and a slice of sun-dried tomato, then garnish with a sprinkling of walnuts and flat-leafed parsley.

EASY		NUTRITIONAL INFORMATION		Makes
Preparation Time 20 minutes, plus chilling	**Cooking Time** 2 minutes	**Per Serving** 208 calories, 9g fat (of which 1g saturates), 24g carbohydrate, 1.7g salt	Dairy free	**15**

Chicken Fajitas

700g (1½lb) skinless chicken breasts, cut into chunky strips
2 tbsp fajita seasoning
1 tbsp sunflower oil
1 red pepper, seeded and sliced
360g jar fajita sauce
1 bunch of spring onions, halved
8 large flour tortillas
150g (5oz) tomato salsa
125g (4oz) guacamole dip
150ml (¼ pint) soured cream

1 Put the chicken breasts into a shallow dish and toss together with the fajita seasoning. Heat the oil in a large, non-stick frying pan, add the chicken and cook for 5 minutes or until golden brown and tender.

2 Add the red pepper and cook for 2 minutes. Pour in the fajita sauce, bring to the boil and simmer for 5 minutes or until thoroughly heated. Add a splash of boiling water if the sauce becomes too thick. Stir in the spring onions and cook for 2 minutes.

3 Meanwhile, warm the tortillas in a microwave on full power for 45 seconds, or wrap in foil and warm in a preheated oven at 180°C (160°C fan oven) mark 4 for 10 minutes.

4 Transfer the chicken to a serving dish and take to the table, along with the tortillas, salsa, guacamole and soured cream. Let everyone help themselves.

EASY		NUTRITIONAL INFORMATION	Serves
Preparation Time 10 minutes	**Cooking Time** 20 minutes	**Per Serving** 651 calories, 23g fat (of which 8g saturates), 63g carbohydrate, 1.6g salt	**4**

2

Soups and Salads

Try Something Different

Use smoked turkey or duck instead of smoked chicken.
For extra flavour, add 2 fresh rosemary sprigs and 2 bay leaves when cooking the lentils, discarding them when you drain the lentils.

Warm Lentil, Chicken and Broccoli Salad

125g (4oz) Puy lentils
225g (8oz) broccoli, chopped
1 large garlic clove, crushed
1 tsp English mustard powder
2 tbsp balsamic vinegar
4 tbsp olive oil
1 red pepper, seeded and sliced into rings
350g (12oz) smoked chicken breast, shredded
salt

1 Put the lentils into a pan and cover generously with boiling water. Cook for 15 minutes or until tender, or according to the pack instructions. Blanch the broccoli in a pan of boiling water for 2 minutes. Drain, refresh under cold water and set aside.

2 Put the garlic into a bowl and use a wooden spoon to combine it with a pinch of salt until creamy, then whisk in the mustard, balsamic vinegar and 3 tbsp olive oil. Set aside.

3 Heat the remaining oil in a frying pan, add the red pepper and cook for 5 minutes or until softened.

4 Add the chicken and broccoli and stir-fry for 1–2 minutes. Stir in the lentils and dressing, and serve warm.

Serves	EASY		NUTRITIONAL INFORMATION	
4	**Preparation Time** 20 minutes	**Cooking Time** 25 minutes	**Per Serving** 332 calories, 16g fat (of which 3g saturates), 22g carbohydrate, 1.6g salt	Gluten free Dairy free

50g (2oz) pecan nuts or walnuts

350g (12oz) smoked chicken or cooked chicken breast, skinned and cut into long strips

2 oranges

2 small chicory heads

For the dressing

grated zest and juice of 2 oranges

2 tbsp white wine vinegar

1 tsp caster sugar

5 tbsp olive oil

3 tbsp freshly chopped tarragon

1 large egg yolk

salt and ground black pepper

Zesty Orange, Chicken and Tarragon Salad

1 Put the nuts into a dry pan and toast over a medium-high heat, tossing regularly, for 2–3 minutes or until golden brown. Chop roughly.

2 Whisk all the dressing ingredients together in a small bowl. Put the chicken strips into a bowl, spoon over the dressing, cover and chill for at least 1 hour.

3 Use a sharp knife to remove the peel and pith from the oranges, then cut into slices.

4 Put a layer of chicory in a large, flat salad bowl and spoon the chicken and dressing over. Scatter on the orange slices and nuts, and serve.

EASY	NUTRITIONAL INFORMATION		Serves
Preparation Time 15 minutes, plus at least 1 hour chilling	**Per Serving** 252 calories, 8g fat (of which 2g saturates), 20g carbohydrate, 0.5g salt	Gluten free Dairy free	**4**

1 tbsp olive oil

1 onion, finely chopped

4 celery sticks, chopped

1 red chilli, seeded and roughly chopped
(see page 23)

2 skinless chicken breasts, about 125g (4oz) each,
cut into strips

1 litre (1³/₄ pints) hot chicken or vegetable stock

100g (3¹/₂oz) bulgur wheat

2 x 400g cans cannellini beans, drained and rinsed

400g can chopped tomatoes

25g (1oz) flat-leafed parsley, roughly chopped

wholegrain bread and hummus to serve

Chicken and Bean Soup

1 Heat the olive oil in a large, heavy-based pan. Add the onion, celery and chilli and cook over a low heat for 10 minutes or until softened. Add the chicken and stir-fry for 3–4 minutes until golden.

2 Add the stock to the pan and bring to a simmer. Stir in the bulgur wheat and then simmer for 15 minutes. Stir in the cannellini beans and tomatoes, and bring to a simmer. Ladle into bowls and sprinkle with chopped parsley. Serve with wholegrain bread and hummus.

Serves	EASY		NUTRITIONAL INFORMATION	
4	**Preparation Time** 10 minutes	**Cooking Time** 30 minutes	**Per Serving** 351 calories, 6g fat (of which 1g saturates), 48g carbohydrate, 2.7g salt	Dairy free

Cook's Tips

As a main course, this soup will serve 4.
Make the stock a day ahead, if possible, then cool overnight. The following day remove any fat from the surface.

Cock-a-Leekie Soup

1 oven-ready chicken, about 1.4kg (3lb)
2 onions, roughly chopped
2 carrots, roughly chopped
2 celery sticks, roughly chopped
1 bay leaf
25g (1oz) butter
900g (2lb) leeks, trimmed and sliced
125g (4oz) ready-to-eat stoned prunes, sliced
salt and ground black pepper
freshly chopped parsley to serve

For the dumplings
125g (4oz) self-raising white flour
a pinch of salt
50g (2oz) shredded suet
2 tbsp freshly chopped parsley
2 tbsp freshly chopped thyme

1 Put the chicken into a pan in which it fits quite snugly. Add the chopped vegetables, bay leaf and chicken giblets (if available). Add 1.7 litres (3 pints) water, bring to the boil, reduce the heat, cover and simmer gently for 1 hour.

2 Meanwhile, melt the butter in a large pan, add the leeks and fry gently for 10 minutes or until softened.

3 Remove the chicken from the pan. Strain the stock and set aside. Strip the chicken from the bones and shred roughly. Add to the stock with the prunes and softened leeks.

4 To make the dumplings, sift the flour and salt into a bowl. Stir in the suet, herbs and about 5 tbsp water to make a fairly firm dough. Lightly shape the dough into 2.5cm (1in) balls. Bring the soup just to the boil and season well. Reduce the heat, add the dumplings and cover the pan with a lid. Simmer for about 15–20 minutes until the dumplings are light and fluffy. Serve scattered with chopped parsley.

EASY		NUTRITIONAL INFORMATION	Serves
Preparation Time 30–40 minutes	**Cooking Time** 1 hour 20 minutes	**Per Serving** 280 calories, 4g fat (of which 1g saturates), 40g carbohydrate, 0.2g salt	**8**

Thai Chicken and Noodle Soup

vegetable oil for shallow or deep-frying

225g (8oz) firm tofu, patted dry and cut into 1cm (½in) cubes

2.5cm (1in) piece fresh root ginger, peeled and finely chopped

2.5cm (1in) piece fresh or dried galangal, peeled and thinly sliced (optional, see Cook's Tip)

1–2 garlic cloves, crushed

2 lemongrass stalks, halved lengthways and bruised (see page 22)

1 tsp chilli powder

½ tsp ground turmeric

275g (10oz) cooked chicken, skinned and cut into bite-size pieces

175g (6oz) cauliflower, broken into small florets and any thick stems thinly sliced

1 large carrot, cut into matchsticks

600ml (1 pint) coconut milk

600ml (1 pint) chicken or vegetable stock, or water

a few green beans, trimmed and halved

125g (4oz) fine or medium egg noodles

125g (4oz) peeled prawns (optional)

3 spring onions, thinly sliced

75g (3oz) beansprouts

2 tbsp soy sauce

1 Heat the oil in a wok or deep-fryer to 180°C (test by frying a small cube of bread; it should brown in 40 seconds). Fry the tofu, in batches, for about 1 minute or until golden brown all over. Drain on kitchen paper.

2 Heat 2 tbsp oil in a large pan. Add the ginger, galangal, if using, garlic, lemongrass, chilli powder, turmeric and chicken. Cook, stirring for 2 minutes.

3 Add the cauliflower, carrot, coconut milk and stock or water. Bring to the boil, stirring all the time. Reduce the heat and simmer for 10 minutes. Add the beans and simmer for 5 minutes.

4 Meanwhile, bring a large pan of water to the boil and cook the noodles for about 4 minutes or according to the pack instructions. Drain the noodles and add them to the soup with the prawns, if using, the tofu, spring onions, beansprouts and soy sauce. Simmer gently for 5 minutes or until heated through. Serve immediately.

Cook's Tip

Dried galangal, similar in flavour to root ginger, needs to be soaked for 30 minutes before using. It's used chopped or grated in many Thai, Indonesian and Malay dishes.

EASY		NUTRITIONAL INFORMATION		Serves
Preparation Time 20 minutes	**Cooking Time** about 30 minutes	**Per Serving** 384 calories, 15g fat (of which 3g saturates), 36g carbohydrate, 2g salt	Dairy free	**4**

Chicken, Avocado and Peanut Salad

2 ready-roasted chicken breasts, about 250g (9oz) total weight, skinned and sliced

75g (3oz) watercress

2 tbsp cider vinegar

1 tsp English ready-made mustard

5 tbsp groundnut oil

1 large ripe avocado, halved, stoned and thickly sliced

50g (2oz) roasted salted peanuts, roughly chopped

salt and ground black pepper

1 Arrange the sliced chicken on top of the watercress, cover with clingfilm and chill until ready to serve.

2 Put the vinegar, mustard and oil together in a bowl, season with salt and pepper and whisk together. Add the avocado and gently toss in the dressing, making sure each slice of avocado is well coated.

3 Just before serving, spoon the avocado and dressing over the chicken and watercress. Sprinkle with the chopped peanuts and serve immediately.

Serves 4	EASY		NUTRITIONAL INFORMATION	
	Preparation Time 15 minutes, plus chilling		**Per Serving** 335 calories, 28g fat (of which 4g saturates), 2g carbohydrate, 0.1g salt	Gluten free Dairy free

1 tbsp olive oil

300g (11oz) boneless, skinless chicken thighs, cubed

3 garlic cloves, crushed

2 medium red chillies, seeded and finely diced (see page 23)

1 litre (1³/₄ pints) chicken stock

250g (9oz) each green beans, broccoli, sugarsnap peas and courgettes, sliced

50g (2oz) vermicelli or spaghetti, broken into short lengths

Chicken Noodle Soup

1 Heat the olive oil in a large pan, add the chicken, garlic and chilli and cook for 5–10 minutes until the chicken is opaque all over.

2 Add the stock, bring to the boil, then add the vegetables and simmer for 5 minutes or until the chicken is cooked through.

3 Meanwhile, cook the pasta in a separate pan of salted boiling water for 5–10 minutes, or until al dente, depending on the type of pasta.

4 Drain the pasta, add to the broth, and serve immediately.

A LITTLE EFFORT		NUTRITIONAL INFORMATION		Serves
Preparation Time 30 minutes	**Cooking Time** 15 minutes	**Per Serving** 229 calories, 7g fat (of which 1g saturates), 16g carbohydrate, 1.2g salt	Dairy free	**4**

Quick Caribbean Chicken Salad

4 chicken breasts, with skin, about 125g (4oz) each

4 tsp jerk seasoning

450g (1lb) Jersey Royal potatoes

100ml (3½fl oz) mayonnaise

2 tbsp wholegrain mustard

2 tbsp vegetable oil

1 red onion, cut into thin wedges

125g (4oz) brown-cap mushrooms, halved

225g (8oz) young spinach leaves

3 tbsp freshly chopped chives

lemon juice to taste

salt and ground black pepper

1 Season the chicken breasts with salt and pepper and rub with jerk seasoning. Heat the grill to high. Grill the chicken breasts for 5 minutes on each side or until cooked through. Set aside.

2 Meanwhile, cook the potatoes in salted boiling water for 10 minutes or until tender. Drain, cool a little, then cut into chunks. Mix the mayonnaise and mustard together, then add to the potatoes, stir and set aside.

3 Heat the oil in a large frying pan, add the onion and fry for 5 minutes. Add the mushrooms and cook for a further 2 minutes, then season with salt and pepper.

4 Combine the potato and mushroom mixtures in a bowl and add the spinach. Toss with the chives, add the lemon juice and season with salt and pepper. Cut the chicken into thick slices on the diagonal and serve with the salad.

Serves	EASY		NUTRITIONAL INFORMATION	
4	**Preparation Time** 10 minutes	**Cooking Time** 17 minutes	**Per Serving** 543 calories, 33g fat (of which 6g saturates), 25g carbohydrate, 0.7g salt	Gluten free Dairy free

Warm Chicken Liver Salad

25g (1oz) butter

450g (1lb) chicken livers, trimmed of sinew and fat, and patted dry

300g (11oz) asparagus tips, trimmed, cooked for 5 minutes in simmering salted water, drained and dried

125g (4oz) wild rocket

75g (3oz) pinenuts, dry fried and cooled

For the dressing

6 small oranges

200ml (7fl oz) light olive oil

4 tbsp red wine vinegar

2 tbsp clear honey

50g (2oz) raisins

salt and ground black pepper

1 To make the dressing, grate the zest from 2 oranges, squeeze the juice and set aside. Peel and segment the remaining 4 oranges and set aside. Pour the olive oil and vinegar into a small pan. Add 6 tbsp of the orange juice (reserving the remainder), the zest, honey and raisins. Season well with salt and pepper, and whisk together. Bring gently to the boil, remove from the heat and set aside.

2 Heat the butter in a large, heavy-based pan and, when the foaming has subsided, add the livers and cook over a high heat for about 5 minutes or until well browned. Remove from the pan and keep warm.

3 Add the remaining orange juice and the dressing to the pan. Allow to bubble for 1–2 minutes, stirring and scraping the pan to dissolve any sediment.

4 Divide the livers, orange segments, asparagus and rocket among six bowls. Scatter the pinenuts on top, spoon the dressing over and finish with a grinding of black pepper. Serve at once.

EASY		NUTRITIONAL INFORMATION		Serves
Preparation Time 10 minutes	**Cooking Time** 15–20 minutes	**Per Serving** 478 calories, 39g fat (of which 7g saturates), 14g carbohydrate, 0.3g salt	Gluten free	**6**

Chargrilled Chicken Waldorf

125g (4oz) walnuts

olive oil to brush

2 skinless chicken breasts, about 125g (4oz) each

100g (3½oz) salad leaves

125g (4oz) black seedless grapes

2 crisp, red apples, such as Braeburn, cored and thinly sliced

4 celery sticks, sliced into matchsticks

175g (6oz) Roquefort cheese, thinly sliced

150ml (¼ pint) mayonnaise

salt and ground black pepper

freshly chopped chives to garnish (optional)

1 Put the walnuts into a dry pan and toast over a medium-high heat, tossing regularly, for 2–3 minutes or until golden brown. Set aside. Brush a griddle or frying pan with a little oil and put over a medium heat. Season the chicken with salt and pepper and cook for about 8–10 minutes on each side until cooked through. Set aside.

2 In a large bowl, toss together the salad leaves, grapes, apples, celery, walnuts and about two-thirds of the Roquefort. Thickly slice the chicken and arrange on four plates with some salad.

3 Crumble the remaining cheese into the mayonnaise and mix well. Spoon 2 tbsp mayonnaise on to each plate, or serve separately, and garnish with the chopped chives, if you like.

EASY		NUTRITIONAL INFORMATION		Serves
Preparation Time 10 minutes	**Cooking Time** 16–20 minutes	**Per Serving** 702 calories, 61g fat (of which 14g saturates), 10g carbohydrate, 1.9g salt	Gluten free	**4**

Spring Chicken Salad with Sweet Chilli Sauce

4 skinless chicken breasts, about 125g (4oz) each, cut into four strips each

1 tbsp Cajun seasoning

2 tbsp groundnut oil, plus extra to grease

Thai chilli dipping sauce to drizzle

salt and ground black pepper

For the salad

175g (6oz) small young carrots, cut into thin matchsticks

125g (4oz) cucumber, halved lengthways, deseeded and cut into matchsticks

6 spring onions, cut into matchsticks

10 radishes, sliced

50g (2oz) beansprouts

50g (2oz) unsalted peanuts, roughly chopped

1 large red chilli, seeded and finely chopped (see page 23)

2 tsp toasted sesame oil

1 Soak eight wooden skewers in water for 20 minutes. Oil a baking sheet. Preheat the grill to high.

2 Toss the chicken strips in the Cajun seasoning, then season with salt and pepper and brush with groundnut oil. Thread on to the skewers.

3 Put the skewered chicken fillets on the baking sheet and cook under the grill for 3–4 minutes on each side until cooked through.

4 Put all the salad vegetables, peanuts and red chilli into a bowl, toss with the sesame oil and season well with salt and pepper.

5 Divide the vegetables among four serving plates, top with the warm chicken skewers and drizzle with the chilli sauce. Serve immediately.

Serves 4	EASY		NUTRITIONAL INFORMATION	
	Preparation Time 15 minutes, plus soaking	**Cooking Time** 10 minutes	**Per Serving** 307 calories, 15g fat (of which 3g saturates), 8g carbohydrate, 0.2g salt	Gluten free Dairy free

grated zest and juice of 1 lemon

4 skinless chicken breasts, about 125g (4oz) each, slashed several times

1 tbsp ground coriander

2 tsp olive oil

For the salad

225g (8oz) bulgur wheat

6 tomatoes, chopped

$^{1}/_{2}$ cucumber, chopped

4 spring onions, chopped

50g (2oz) dried dates, chopped

50g (2oz) almonds, chopped

3 tbsp freshly chopped flat-leafed parsley

3 tbsp freshly chopped mint

salt and ground black pepper

Chicken with Bulgur Wheat Salad

1 Put half the lemon zest and juice into a bowl, then add the chicken breasts, coriander and 1 tsp oil. Toss well to mix. Leave to marinate while you prepare the salad. Preheat the grill to high.

2 To make the salad, cook the bulgur wheat according to the pack instructions (about 10 minutes, see page 27). Put into a bowl, add the remaining salad ingredients and season well with salt and pepper. Add the remaining lemon zest, juice and oil and stir well.

3 Grill the chicken for 10 minutes on each side or until cooked through. The juices should run clear when the meat is pierced with a sharp knife. Slice the chicken and serve with the salad.

EASY		NUTRITIONAL INFORMATION		Serves
Preparation Time 20 minutes, plus marinating	**Cooking Time** 30 minutes	**Per Serving** 429 calories, 12g fat (of which 1g saturates), 45g carbohydrate, 0.2g salt	Dairy free	**4**

Cook's Tip

Egg shells and whites are used to make soups, such as consommé, clear. When heated slowly, they trap the impurities as they coagulate, forming a scum layer on the top of the soup. Once the layer of scum has formed, the soup is gently strained through kitchen paper or a cloth, leaving behind a clear soup.

1.7 litres (3 pints) well-flavoured fat-free chicken stock

350g (12oz) skinless chicken breast, minced

2 leeks, trimmed and thinly sliced

2 celery sticks, thinly sliced

2 carrots, thinly sliced

2 shallots, diced

2 medium egg whites, lightly whisked

2 medium egg shells, crushed (see Cook's Tip)

a dash of sherry or Madeira (optional)

salt and ground black pepper

Chicken Consommé

1 Heat the stock in a pan. Combine the chicken and vegetables in another large pan, then mix in the egg whites and shells.

2 Gradually whisk in the hot stock, then bring to the boil, whisking. As soon as it comes to the boil, stop whisking, lower the heat and simmer very gently for 1 hour. By this time, a crust will have formed on the surface and the stock underneath should be clear.

3 Carefully make a hole in the crust and ladle the clear stock out into a muslin-lined sieve over a large bowl. Allow to drain through slowly, then put back into the cleaned pan and reheat. Check the seasoning and flavour with a little sherry or Madeira, if you like.

Serves	A LITTLE EFFORT		NUTRITIONAL INFORMATION	
4	**Preparation Time** 30 minutes	**Cooking Time** 1¼ hours	**Per Serving** 18 calories, 1g fat, 1g carbohydrate, 3.1g salt	Gluten free Dairy free

Chicken Caesar Salad

2 tbsp olive oil
1 garlic clove, crushed
2 thick slices of country-style bread, cubed
6 tbsp freshly grated Parmesan
1 cos lettuce, chilled and cut into bite-size pieces
700g (1½lb) cooked chicken breast, sliced

For the dressing
4 tbsp mayonnaise
2 tbsp lemon juice
1 tsp Dijon mustard
2 anchovy fillets, very finely chopped
salt and ground black pepper

1 Preheat the oven to 180°C (160°C fan oven) mark 4. Put the olive oil, garlic and bread cubes into a bowl and toss well. Tip on to a baking sheet and cook in the oven for 10 minutes, turning halfway through.

2 Sprinkle the Parmesan over the croûtons and cook for 2 minutes or until the cheese has melted and the bread is golden.

3 Put all the dressing ingredients into a bowl, season with salt and pepper and mix.

4 Put the lettuce and sliced chicken into a bowl, pour the dressing over and toss. Top with the cheese croûtons.

EASY		NUTRITIONAL INFORMATION	Serves
Preparation Time 15–20 minutes	**Cooking Time** 12 minutes	**Per Serving** 498 calories, 31g fat (of which 9g saturates), 7g carbohydrate, 1.4g salt	**4**

Warm Chicken Salad with Quick Hollandaise

1 tbsp white wine vinegar
1 tbsp lemon juice
1 tbsp olive oil
3 chicken breasts, with skin, about 125g (4oz) each
150g (5oz) asparagus tips, trimmed
2 large egg yolks
125g (4oz) unsalted butter, melted
200g (7oz) baby salad leaves with herbs
salt and ground black pepper
lemon wedges to serve

1 Put the vinegar and lemon juice into a small pan over a medium heat. Bring to the boil and simmer to reduce by half. Leave to cool slightly.

2 Heat a griddle until hot and brush with the olive oil. Put the chicken on a board, cover with clingfilm and gently flatten with a rolling pin. Remove the clingfilm, season with salt and pepper and griddle for about 8 minutes on each side or until cooked through. Keep warm.

3 Bring a large pan of lightly salted water to the boil. Cook the asparagus for 2–3 minutes until tender. Drain and keep warm.

4 Meanwhile, whiz the yolks in a blender for a few seconds until thickened. With the blender running, pour the reduced vinegar mixture slowly on to the eggs, then gradually add the melted butter – the mixture will start to thicken. If it's too thick, blend in a little hot water to loosen.

5 Cut the chicken into slices and divide among four plates with the asparagus and salad leaves. Serve with the hollandaise for drizzling and lemon wedges to squeeze over.

Serves 4	EASY		NUTRITIONAL INFORMATION	
	Preparation Time 15 minutes	**Cooking Time** about 20 minutes	**Per Serving** 411 calories, 34g fat (of which 19g saturates), 2g carbohydrate, 0.8g salt	Gluten free

3

Simple Suppers

Pesto Roast Chicken

20g (³/₄oz) fresh basil, roughly chopped

25g (1oz) freshly grated Parmesan

50g (2oz) pinenuts

4 tbsp extra virgin olive oil

1 chicken, about 1.4kg (3lb)

salt and ground black pepper

new or roast potatoes, and green vegetables to serve

1 Preheat the oven to 200°C (180°C fan oven) mark 6. To make the pesto, put the basil, Parmesan, pinenuts and olive oil into a food processor and mix to a rough paste. (Alternatively, grind the ingredients using a mortar and pestle.) Season with salt and pepper.

2 Put the chicken into a roasting tin. Ease your fingers under the skin of the neck end to separate the breast skin from the flesh, then push about three-quarters of the pesto under the skin, using your hands to spread it evenly. Smear the remainder over the chicken legs. Season with pepper and roast for 1 hour 25 minutes or until the chicken is cooked and the juices run clear when the thickest part of the thigh is pierced with a skewer.

3 Put the chicken on a board, cover with foil and leave to rest for 15 minutes. Carve and serve with potatoes and green vegetables.

Serves	EASY		NUTRITIONAL INFORMATION	
4	**Preparation Time** 10 minutes	**Cooking Time** about 1 hour 25 minutes, plus resting	**Per Serving** 715 calories, 58g fat (of which 14g saturates), 1g carbohydrate, 0.6g salt	Gluten free

6 tbsp vegetable oil

450g (1lb) skinless chicken breasts, cut into bite-size pieces

3 tbsp oyster sauce

1 tbsp dark soy sauce

100ml (3½fl oz) chicken stock

2 tsp lemon juice

1 garlic clove, thinly sliced

6–8 large flat mushrooms, about 250g (9oz) total weight, sliced

125g (4oz) mangetouts

1 tsp cornflour mixed with 1 tbsp water

1 tbsp toasted sesame oil

salt and ground black pepper

rice to serve

Chicken with Oyster Sauce

1 Heat 3 tbsp vegetable oil in a wok or large frying pan. Add the chicken and cook over a high heat, stirring continuously for 2–3 minutes until lightly browned. Remove the chicken with a slotted spoon and drain on kitchen paper.

2 In a bowl, mix the oyster sauce with the soy sauce, chicken stock and lemon juice. Add the chicken and mix thoroughly.

3 Heat the remaining vegetable oil in the pan over a high heat and stir-fry the garlic for about 30 seconds; add the mushrooms and cook for 1 minute. Add the chicken mixture, cover and simmer for 8 minutes.

4 Stir in the mangetouts and cook for a further 2–3 minutes. Remove the pan from the heat and stir in the cornflour mixture. Put the pan back on the heat, add the sesame oil and stir until the sauce has thickened. Season with salt and pepper and serve immediately with rice.

EASY		NUTRITIONAL INFORMATION		Serves
Preparation Time 10 minutes,	**Cooking Time** about 18 minutes	**Per Serving** 344 calories, 23g fat (of which 3g saturates), 7g carbohydrate, 1.1g salt	Dairy free	**4**

Chicken with Vegetables and Noodles

225g (8oz) fine egg noodles

about 2 tbsp vegetable oil

1 large skinless chicken breast, about 150g (5oz), cut into very thin strips

2.5cm (1in) piece fresh root ginger, peeled and finely chopped

1 garlic clove, finely chopped

1 red pepper, seeded and thinly sliced

4 spring onions, thinly sliced

2 carrots, thinly sliced

125g (4oz) shiitake or button mushrooms, halved

a handful of beansprouts (optional)

3 tbsp hoisin sauce

2 tbsp light soy sauce

1 tbsp chilli sauce

shredded spring onion and sesame seeds to garnish

1 Bring a large pan of water to the boil and cook the noodles for about 3 minutes or according to the pack instructions. Drain thoroughly and toss with a little of the oil to prevent them sticking together. Set aside.

2 Heat the remaining oil in a wok or large frying pan. Add the chicken, ginger and garlic, and stir-fry over a very high heat for about 5 minutes, or until the chicken is browned on the outside and cooked right through.

3 Add all the vegetables to the pan and stir-fry over a high heat for about 2 minutes or until they are just cooked, but still crunchy.

4 Stir in the hoisin, soy and chilli sauces, and mix well. Add the noodles, toss well to mix and cook for a couple of minutes until heated through. Serve immediately, sprinkled with shredded spring onion and sesame seeds.

Try Something Different

Replace the chicken with thinly sliced turkey escalopes.
Increase the heat of the dish by frying a chopped chilli with the garlic and ginger.

EASY		NUTRITIONAL INFORMATION		Serves
Preparation Time 10 minutes	**Cooking Time** about 12 minutes	**Per Serving** 584 calories, 19g fat (of which 3g saturates), 67g carbohydrate, 4.1g salt	Dairy free	**2**

4 small skinless chicken breasts, about 125g (4oz) each, cut into chunky strips

juice of 2 lemons

2 tbsp olive oil

4–6 tbsp demerara sugar

salt

green salad to serve

Lemon Chicken

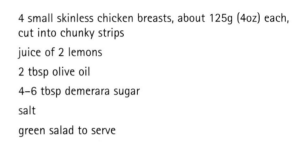

1 Put the chicken into a large bowl and season with salt. Add the lemon juice and olive oil and stir to mix.

2 Preheat the grill to medium. Spread the chicken out on a large baking sheet, and sprinkle over 2–3 tbsp demerara sugar. Grill for 3–4 minutes until caramelised, then turn the chicken over, sprinkle with the remaining sugar and grill until the chicken is cooked through and golden.

3 Divide the chicken among four plates, and serve with a green salad.

Serves	EASY		NUTRITIONAL INFORMATION	
4	**Preparation Time** 2 minutes	**Cooking Time** 6–8 minutes	**Per Serving** 231 calories, 7g fat (of which 1g saturates), 13g carbohydrate, 0.2g salt	Gluten free

Try Something Different

- -

Use chopped black olives instead of the capers.

Mediterranean Chicken

1 red pepper, seeded and chopped

2 tbsp capers

2 tbsp freshly chopped rosemary

2 tbsp olive oil

4 skinless chicken breasts, about 125g (4oz) each

salt and ground black pepper

rice or new potatoes to serve

1 Preheat the oven to 200°C (180°C fan oven) mark 6. Put the red pepper into a bowl with the capers, rosemary and olive oil. Season with salt and pepper and mix well.

2 Put the chicken breasts into an ovenproof dish and spoon the pepper mixture over the top. Roast for 15–20 minutes until the chicken is cooked through and the topping is hot. Serve with rice or new potatoes.

EASY		NUTRITIONAL INFORMATION		Serves
Preparation Time 5 minutes	**Cooking Time** 20 minutes	**Per Serving** 223 calories, 7g fat (of which 1g saturates), 3g carbohydrate, 0.2g salt	Gluten free Dairy free	**4**

Chicken with Mango Salsa

1 tbsp olive oil

4 chicken breasts, with skin, about 125g (4oz) each

salt and ground black pepper

rocket leaves to serve

For the salsa

1 mango, peeled, stoned and diced

1 small fennel bulb, diced

1 fresh chilli, seeded and finely diced (see page 23)

1 tbsp balsamic vinegar

juice of 1 lime

2 tbsp freshly chopped flat-leafed parsley

2 tbsp freshly chopped mint

1 Heat the olive oil in a frying pan. Season the chicken generously with salt and pepper and cook in the pan, skin side down, for 8–10 minutes. Turn over and continue to cook on the other side for 8–10 minutes until cooked through and the juices run clear when the chicken is pierced with a sharp knife. Set aside.

2 Combine all the salsa ingredients in a bowl and season generously with salt and pepper. Spoon alongside the chicken and serve with rocket leaves.

Serves 4	EASY		NUTRITIONAL INFORMATION	
	Preparation Time 10 minutes	**Cooking Time** 20 minutes	**Per Serving** 288 calories, 14g fat (of which 4g saturates), 7g carbohydrate, 0.2g salt	Gluten free Dairy free

Cook's Tip

Quinoa is a tiny, bead-shaped grain with a slightly nutty flavour. It's easy to prepare, and nearly quadruples in size and looks translucent when cooked. It can be substituted for rice or couscous.

2 tbsp mango chutney

juice of ½ lemon

1 tbsp olive oil

2 tsp mild curry powder

1 tsp paprika

350g (12oz) skinless chicken breast, cut into thick strips

200g (7oz) quinoa (see Cook's Tip)

1 cucumber, roughly chopped

½ bunch of spring onions, sliced

75g (3oz) ready-to-eat dried apricots, sliced

2 tbsp freshly chopped mint, basil or tarragon

salt and ground black pepper

Mild Spiced Chicken and Quinoa

1 Put the chutney, lemon juice, ½ tbsp olive oil, the curry powder, paprika and salt and pepper into a bowl and mix together. Add the chicken and toss to coat.

2 Cook the quinoa in boiling water for 10–12 minutes until tender (or according to the pack instructions). Drain thoroughly. Put into a bowl, then stir in the cucumber, spring onions, apricots, herbs and remaining oil.

3 Put the chicken and marinade into a pan and fry over a high heat for 2–3 minutes, then add 150ml (¼ pint) water. Bring to the boil, then simmer for 5 minutes or until the chicken is cooked through. Serve with the quinoa.

A LITTLE EFFORT		NUTRITIONAL INFORMATION		Serves
Preparation Time 15 minutes	**Cooking Time** 20 minutes	**Per Serving** 268 calories, 3g fat (of which trace saturates), 37g carbohydrate, 0.4g salt	Gluten free Dairy free	4

Peas and Bacon with Pan-fried Chicken

4 skinless chicken breasts, about 125g (4oz) each

2 tbsp olive oil

2 shallots, finely sliced

3 unsmoked, rindless streaky bacon rashers, chopped

200g (7oz) frozen peas, thawed

2 tbsp sunblush tomato pesto

salt and ground black pepper

buttered new potatoes to serve

1 Heat a griddle. Season the chicken generously with salt and pepper. Brush with 1 tbsp olive oil and cook on the griddle, skin side down, for 8–10 minutes. Turn over and continue to cook on the other side for 8–10 minutes until cooked through and the juices run clear when the chicken is pierced with a sharp knife.

2 Meanwhile, heat the remaining oil in a frying pan and fry the shallots and bacon until the shallots are softened and the bacon is golden. Add the thawed peas and cook for 2 minutes.

3 Stir in the pesto. Serve with the chicken breasts and new potatoes.

Serves	EASY		NUTRITIONAL INFORMATION	
4	**Preparation Time** 5 minutes	**Cooking Time** 20 minutes	**Per Serving** 314 calories, 21g fat (of which 5g saturates), 7g carbohydrate, 0.9g salt	Gluten free Dairy free

Try Something Different

To use leftover chicken or turkey, don't fry the meat at step 2. Add it to the pan with the crème fraîche at step 3. Cook the leeks in 2 tsp olive oil.

For a different flavour, make the mash with 2 large potatoes and a small celeriac, peeled, cut into chunks and cooked with the potato.

Chicken and Leek Pie

5 large potatoes, peeled and chopped into chunks

200g (7oz) crème fraîche

3 chicken breasts, with skin, about 125g (4oz) each

3 large leeks, trimmed and chopped into chunks

about 10 fresh tarragon leaves, finely chopped

salt and ground black pepper

1 Preheat the oven to 200°C (180°C fan oven) mark 6. Put the potatoes into a pan of salted cold water. Cover, bring to the boil and simmer for 10–12 minutes until soft. Drain and put back in the pan. Add 1 tbsp crème fraîche, season with salt and pepper, and mash well.

2 Meanwhile, heat a frying pan, add the chicken, skin side down, and fry gently for 5 minutes or until the skin is golden. Turn the chicken over and fry for 6–8 minutes. Remove the chicken from the pan and put on to a board. Tip the leeks into the pan and cook in the juices over a low heat for 5 minutes to soften.

3 Discard the chicken skin and cut the flesh into bite-size pieces (don't worry if it is not quite cooked through). Put the chicken back into the pan, stir in the remaining crème fraîche and heat for 2–3 minutes until bubbling. Stir in the tarragon, season with salt and pepper, then spoon into a 1.7 litre (3 pint) ovenproof dish. Spread the mash on top and cook in the oven for 20–25 minutes until golden and heated through. Serve hot.

Serves 4	EASY		NUTRITIONAL INFORMATION	
	Preparation Time 15 minutes	**Cooking Time** 40–45 minutes	**Per Serving** 591 calories, 23g fat (of which 15g saturates), 54g carbohydrate, 0.3g salt	Gluten free

Try Something Different

Replace the chicken with pork escalopes or rump steak, cut into thin strips.

Chicken with Peanut Sauce

4 skinless chicken breasts, about 125g (4oz) each, cut into strips

1 tbsp ground coriander

2 garlic cloves, finely chopped

about 4 tbsp vegetable oil

2 tbsp clear honey

Thai fragrant rice to serve

fresh coriander sprigs to garnish

For the peanut sauce

1 tbsp vegetable oil

2 tbsp curry paste

2 tbsp brown sugar

2 tbsp peanut butter

200ml (7fl oz) coconut milk

1 Mix the chicken with the ground coriander, garlic, oil and honey. Cover, chill and leave to marinate for 15 minutes.

2 To make the peanut sauce, heat the oil in a pan and add the curry paste, brown sugar and peanut butter. Fry for 1 minute. Add the coconut milk and bring to the boil, stirring all the time, then simmer for 5 minutes.

3 Meanwhile, heat a wok or large frying pan and, when hot, stir-fry the chicken and its marinade in batches for 3–4 minutes or until cooked through, adding more oil if needed.

4 Serve the chicken with Thai fragrant rice and the peanut sauce poured over. Garnish with fresh coriander sprigs.

EASY		NUTRITIONAL INFORMATION		Serves
Preparation Time 10 minutes, plus 15 minutes marinating	**Cooking Time** about 10 minutes	**Per Serving** 408 calories, 20g fat (of which 3g saturates), 19g carbohydrate, 0.5g salt	Gluten free Dairy free	**4**

Orange and Herb Chicken

125ml (4fl oz) orange juice

grated zest of 1 unwaxed orange

2 tbsp freshly chopped tarragon

2 tbsp freshly chopped flat-leafed parsley

1 tbsp olive oil

1 garlic clove, crushed

4 skinless chicken breasts, about 125g (4oz) each

4 small orange wedges

salt and ground black pepper

brown rice and watercress to serve

1 Preheat the oven to 200°C (180°C fan oven) mark 6. In a large bowl, whisk together the orange juice, orange zest, herbs, olive oil and garlic. Season with salt and pepper.

2 Slash the chicken breasts several times and put into an ovenproof dish. Pour the marinade over them and top each with an orange wedge.

3 Cook in the oven for 20–30 minutes until cooked through. Serve with brown rice and watercress.

Serves	EASY		NUTRITIONAL INFORMATION	
	Preparation Time	**Cooking Time**	**Per Serving**	
4	10 minutes	20–30 minutes	180 calories, 4g fat (of which 1g saturates), 5g carbohydrate, 0.2g salt	Gluten free Dairy free

125g (4oz) couscous

1 ripe mango, peeled, stoned and cut into 2.5cm (1in) chunks

1 tbsp lemon or lime juice

125g tub fresh tomato salsa

3 tbsp mango chutney

3 tbsp orange juice

2 tbsp freshly chopped coriander, plus extra to garnish

200g (7oz) chargrilled chicken fillets

4 tbsp fromage frais

salt and ground black pepper

lime wedges to garnish

Chicken with Spicy Couscous

1 Put the couscous into a large bowl and pour over 300ml (½ pint) boiling water. Season well with salt and pepper, then leave to stand for 15 minutes.

2 Put the mango on a plate and sprinkle with the lemon or lime juice.

3 Mix together the tomato salsa, mango chutney, orange juice and coriander in a small bowl.

4 Drain the couscous if necessary, fluff the grains with a fork, then stir in the salsa mixture and check the seasoning. Turn out on to a large serving dish, and arrange the chicken and mango on top.

5 Just before serving, spoon the fromage frais over the chicken, then garnish with chopped coriander and lime wedges.

EASY	NUTRITIONAL INFORMATION	Serves
Preparation Time 15 minutes, plus 15 minutes soaking	**Per Serving** 223 calories, 6g fat (of which 2g saturates), 30g carbohydrate, 0.2g salt	**4**

Chicken, Bacon and Leek Pasta Bake

1 tbsp olive oil

100g (3½oz) bacon lardons

450g (1lb) boneless, skinless chicken thighs, chopped

3 medium leeks, trimmed and chopped

300g (11oz) macaroni or other pasta shapes

350g carton ready-made cheese sauce

2 tsp Dijon mustard

2 tbsp freshly chopped flat-leafed parsley

25g (1oz) freshly grated Parmesan

1 Heat the olive oil in a large frying pan. Add the bacon and chicken and cook for 7–8 minutes. Add the leeks and continue cooking for 4–5 minutes.

2 Meanwhile, cook the pasta according to the pack instructions. Drain well.

3 Preheat the grill. Add the cheese sauce to the pasta with the mustard, chicken mixture and parsley. Mix well, then tip into a 2.1 litre (3¾ pint) ovenproof dish and sprinkle with Parmesan. Grill for 4–5 minutes until golden.

EASY		NUTRITIONAL INFORMATION	Serves
Preparation Time 10 minutes	**Cooking Time** about 20 minutes	**Per Serving** 650 calories, 24g fat (of which 6g saturates), 68g carbohydrate, 2.2g salt	**4**

Chicken with Black-eyed Beans and Greens

2 tsp Jamaican jerk seasoning

4 skinless chicken breasts, about 125g (4oz) each

1kg (2¼lb) spring greens or cabbage, core removed and shredded

2 x 300g cans black-eyed beans, drained and rinsed

8 tbsp olive oil

juice of 1¼ lemons

salt and ground black pepper

1 Preheat the grill. Rub the jerk seasoning into the chicken breasts, and sprinkle with salt. Cook under the grill for 15 minutes or until cooked through, turning from time to time.

2 Cook the spring greens or cabbage in salted boiling water until just tender – bringing the water back to the boil after adding the greens is usually enough to cook them. Drain and put back into the pan.

3 Add the beans and olive oil to the greens and season well with salt and pepper. Heat through and add the juice of 1 lemon.

4 To serve, slice the chicken and put on the bean mixture, then drizzle over the remaining lemon juice and serve.

Serves	EASY		NUTRITIONAL INFORMATION	
4	**Preparation Time** 5 minutes	**Cooking Time** 15 minutes	**Per Serving** 491 calories, 26g fat (of which 4g saturates), 31g carbohydrate, 1.5g salt	Gluten free Dairy free

Chicken Rarebit

4 large chicken breasts, with skin, about 150g (5oz) each

15g (½oz) butter

1 tbsp plain flour

75ml (2½fl oz) full-fat milk

175g (6oz) Gruyère cheese, grated

25g (1oz) fresh white breadcrumbs

1 tsp ready-made English mustard

2 fat garlic cloves, crushed

1 medium egg yolk

boiled new potatoes and green beans to serve

1 Preheat the oven to 200°C (180°C fan oven) mark 6. Put the chicken in a single layer into an ovenproof dish and roast for 20 minutes or until cooked through.

2 Meanwhile, melt the butter in a pan over a low heat, then add the flour and stir for 1 minute. Gradually add the milk and stir to make a smooth sauce.

3 Add the cheese, breadcrumbs, mustard and garlic to the sauce and cook for 1 minute. Cool briefly, then beat in the egg yolk. Preheat the grill to medium-high.

4 Discard the skin from the cooked chicken and beat any juices from the dish into the cheese mixture. Spread the paste evenly over each chicken breast, then grill for 2–3 minutes until golden. Serve with boiled new potatoes and green beans.

EASY		NUTRITIONAL INFORMATION	Serves
Preparation Time 5 minutes	**Cooking Time** 25 minutes	**Per Serving** 446 calories, 24g fat (of which 14g saturates), 9g carbohydrate, 1.3g salt	**4**

Chicken Chow Mein

250g (9oz) medium egg noodles

1 tbsp toasted sesame oil

2 skinless chicken breasts, about 125g (4oz) each, cut into thin strips

1 bunch of spring onions, thinly sliced diagonally

150g (5oz) mangetouts, thickly sliced diagonally

125g (4oz) beansprouts

100g (3½oz) cooked ham, finely shredded

120g sachet chow mein sauce

salt and ground black pepper

light soy sauce to serve

1 Cook the noodles in boiling water for 4 minutes or according to the pack instructions. Drain, rinse thoroughly in cold water, drain again and set aside.

2 Meanwhile, heat a wok or large frying pan until hot, then add the sesame oil. Add the chicken and stir-fry over a high heat for 3–4 minutes until browned all over. Add the spring onions and mangetouts, stir-fry for 2 minutes, then stir in the beansprouts and ham. Cook for a further 2 minutes.

3 Add the drained noodles, then pour over the chow mein sauce and toss together to coat evenly. Stir-fry for 2 minutes or until piping hot. Season with salt and pepper, and serve immediately with light soy sauce to drizzle over.

Serves 4	EASY		NUTRITIONAL INFORMATION	
	Preparation Time 10 minutes	**Cooking Time** 10 minutes	**Per Serving** 451 calories, 11g fat (of which 2g saturates), 59g carbohydrate, 1.3g salt	Dairy free

Spiced Chicken with Garlic Butter Beans

4 skinless chicken breasts, about 100g (3½oz) each

1 tbsp olive oil

1 tsp ground cumin

1 tsp ground coriander

100g (3½oz) couscous

3 tbsp extra virgin olive oil

1 garlic clove, sliced

2 x 400g cans butter beans, drained and rinsed

juice of 1 lemon

1 small red onion, thinly sliced

50g (2oz) marinated roasted peppers, drained and chopped

2 tomatoes, seeded and chopped

1 tbsp freshly chopped coriander

1 tbsp freshly chopped flat-leafed parsley

salt and ground black pepper

lemon wedges to serve

1 Put the chicken on a board, cover with clingfilm and flatten lightly with a rolling pin. Put the olive oil into a large bowl and add the spices. Mix together, then add the chicken and turn to coat.

2 Heat a large frying pan and cook the chicken for 5–7 minutes on each side until golden and the juices run clear when the chicken is pierced with a skewer.

3 While the chicken is cooking, put the couscous into a bowl and add 100ml (3½fl oz) boiling water. Cover with clingfilm and set aside.

4 Put the extra virgin olive oil into a small pan with the garlic and butter beans, and warm together for 3–4 minutes over a low heat. Stir in the lemon juice and season with salt and pepper.

5 Fluff up the couscous with a fork and tip in the warm butter beans. Add the remaining ingredients and stir together. Slice each chicken breast and serve with the bean salad and lemon wedges.

EASY		NUTRITIONAL INFORMATION		Serves
Preparation Time 10 minutes	**Cooking Time** about 15 minutes	**Per Serving** 338 calories, 7g fat (of which 2g saturates), 37g carbohydrate, 1.8g salt	Gluten free Dairy free	**4**

4

Curries and Casseroles

One-pot Chicken

2 tbsp olive oil

1 large onion, cut into wedges

2 rindless streaky bacon rashers, chopped

1 chicken, about 1.6kg (3½lb)

6 carrots

2 small turnips, cut into wedges

1 garlic clove, crushed

bouquet garni (1 bay leaf, few fresh parsley and thyme sprigs)

600ml (1 pint) hot chicken stock

100ml (3½fl oz) dry white wine

12 button mushrooms

3 tbsp freshly chopped flat-leafed parsley

salt and ground black pepper

mashed potatoes to serve

1 Heat the olive oil in a non-stick flameproof casserole, then add the onion and bacon, and fry for 5 minutes or until golden. Remove and set aside.

2 Add the whole chicken to the casserole and fry for 10 minutes, turning carefully to brown all over. Remove and set aside.

3 Preheat the oven to 200°C (180°C fan oven) mark 6. Add the carrots, turnips and garlic to the casserole. Fry for 5 minutes, then add the bacon and onion. Put the chicken back into the casserole. Add the bouquet garni, stock and wine. Season with salt and pepper. Bring to a simmer, then cover and cook in the oven for 30 minutes.

4 Remove the casserole from the oven and add the mushrooms. Baste the chicken, then re-cover and cook for a further 50 minutes.

5 Lift out the chicken, then stir the parsley into the cooking liquid. Carve the chicken and serve with the vegetables, cooking liquid and mashed potatoes.

Try Something Different

Use chicken pieces such as drumsticks or thighs, reducing the cooking time in step 4 to 20 minutes.

EASY		NUTRITIONAL INFORMATION		Serves
Preparation Time 20 minutes	**Cooking Time** 1 hour 40 minutes	**Per Serving** 474 calories, 33g fat (of which 9g saturates), 6g carbohydrate, 0.6g salt	Dairy free Gluten Free	**6**

Try Something Different

Use flageolet beans or other canned beans instead of mixed beans, and garnish with fresh basil or oregano.

One-pan Chicken with Tomatoes

4 chicken thighs

1 red onion, sliced

400g can chopped tomatoes with herbs

400g can mixed beans, drained and rinsed

2 tsp balsamic vinegar

freshly chopped flat-leafed parsley to garnish

1 Heat a non-stick pan and fry the chicken thighs, skin side down, until golden. Turn over and fry for 5 minutes.

2 Add the onion and fry for 5 minutes. Add the tomatoes, mixed beans and vinegar, cover and simmer for 10–12 minutes until piping hot. Garnish with parsley and serve immediately.

Serves	EASY		NUTRITIONAL INFORMATION	
4	**Preparation Time** 5 minutes	**Cooking Time** 20–25 minutes	**Per Serving** 238 calories, 4g fat (of which 1g saturates), 20g carbohydrate, 1g salt	Gluten free Dairy free

1 tbsp vegetable oil

3 tbsp Thai red curry paste

4 skinless chicken breasts, about 600g (1lb 5oz) total weight, sliced

400ml can coconut milk

300ml (½ pint) hot chicken or vegetable stock

juice of 1 lime, plus lime halves to serve

200g pack mixed baby sweetcorn and mangetouts

2 tbsp freshly chopped coriander, plus sprigs to garnish

rice or rice noodles to serve

Easy Thai Red Chicken Curry

1 Heat the oil in a wok or large pan over a low heat. Add the curry paste and cook for 2 minutes or until fragrant.

2 Add the sliced chicken and fry gently for about 10 minutes or until browned.

3 Add the coconut milk, stock, lime juice and baby sweetcorn to the pan and bring to the boil. Add the mangetouts, reduce the heat and simmer for 4–5 minutes until the chicken is cooked. Stir in the chopped coriander, garnish with coriander sprigs, and serve immediately with rice or noodles, and lime halves to squeeze over.

EASY		NUTRITIONAL INFORMATION		Serves
Preparation Time 5 minutes	**Cooking Time** 20 minutes	**Per Serving** 248 calories, 8g fat (of which 1g saturates), 16g carbohydrate, 1g salt	Dairy free Gluten Free	**4**

1 tbsp olive oil

4 chicken thighs

1 onion, finely chopped

1 fennel bulb, finely chopped

juice of ½ lemon

200ml (7fl oz) hot chicken stock

200ml (7fl oz) crème fraîche

1 small bunch of tarragon, roughly chopped

salt and ground black pepper

new potatoes and broccoli to serve

Tarragon Chicken with Fennel

1 Preheat the oven to 200°C (180°C fan oven) mark 6. Heat the olive oil in a large, flameproof casserole over a medium-high heat. Add the chicken thighs and fry for 5 minutes or until browned, then remove and put them to one side to keep warm.

2 Add the onion to the casserole and fry for 5 minutes, then add the fennel and cook for 5–10 minutes until softened.

3 Add the lemon juice to the casserole, followed by the stock. Bring to a simmer and cook until the sauce is reduced by half.

4 Stir in the crème fraîche and put the chicken back into the casserole. Stir once to mix, then cover and cook in the oven for 25–30 minutes. Stir the tarragon into the sauce, season with salt and pepper, and serve with potatoes and broccoli.

Serves 4	EASY		NUTRITIONAL INFORMATION	
	Preparation Time 10 minutes	**Cooking Time** 45–55 minutes	**Per Serving** 334 calories, 26g fat (of which 15g saturates), 3g carbohydrate, 0.5g salt	Gluten free

Cook's Tip

Queen green olives are large, meaty olives with a mild flavour. Remember to tell people the olives still have stones.

Spanish Chicken Parcels

12 boneless, skinless chicken thighs, about 900g (2lb)

180g jar pimientos or roasted red peppers, drained

12 thin slices chorizo sausage

2 tbsp olive oil

1 onion, finely chopped

4 garlic cloves, crushed

225g can chopped tomatoes

4 tbsp dry sherry

18 Queen green olives (see Cook's Tip)

salt and ground black pepper

rice or crusty bread to serve

1 Put the chicken thighs on a board, season well with salt and pepper and put a piece of pimiento or roasted pepper inside each one. Wrap a slice of chorizo around the outside and secure with two cocktail sticks. Set aside.

2 Heat the olive oil in a pan over a medium heat and fry the onion for 10 minutes. Add the garlic and cook for 1 minute. Put the chicken parcels, chorizo side down, into the pan and brown them all over for 10–15 minutes.

3 Add the chopped tomatoes and sherry to the pan and bring to the boil. Simmer for 5 minutes or until the juices run clear when the chicken is pierced with a skewer. Add the olives and warm through. Remove the cocktail sticks and serve with rice or crusty bread.

EASY		NUTRITIONAL INFORMATION		Serves
Preparation Time 15 minutes	**Cooking Time** about 30 minutes	**Per Serving** 444 calories, 29g fat (of which 9g saturates), 4g carbohydrate, 3.1g salt	Gluten free Dairy free	**6**

Cook's Tip

Beurre manié is a mixture of equal parts of softened butter and flour that has been kneaded together to form a paste. It's used to thicken sauces and stews. It's whisked in towards the end of cooking, then boiled briefly to allow it to thicken.

Coq au Vin

750ml bottle full-bodied white wine, such as Burgundy or Chardonnay

4 tbsp brandy

2 bouquet garni (bay leaves, fresh parsley and thyme sprigs)

1 garlic clove, bruised

flour to coat

1 chicken, about 1.4kg (3lb), jointed (see page 10), or 2 boneless breasts, halved, plus 2 drumsticks and 2 thighs

125g (4oz) butter

125g (4oz) rindless unsmoked bacon rashers, cut into strips

225g (8oz) baby onions, peeled with root ends intact

225g (8oz) brown-cap mushrooms, halved, or quartered if large

salt and ground black pepper

buttered noodles or rice to serve

For the beurre manié

25g (1oz) butter mixed with 25g (1oz) plain flour

1 Preheat the oven to 180°C (160°C fan oven) mark 4. Pour the wine and brandy into a pan and add 1 bouquet garni and the garlic. Bring to the boil and simmer until reduced by half. Allow to cool.

2 Season the flour with salt and pepper and use to coat the chicken joints lightly. Melt half the butter in a large frying pan. When foaming, add the chicken joints and brown all over (in batches if necessary). Transfer to a flameproof casserole. Add the bacon to the frying pan and fry until golden. Remove with a slotted spoon and add to the chicken.

3 Strain the cooled, reduced wine mixture over the chicken and add the other bouquet garni. Bring to the boil, cover and cook in the oven for 30 minutes.

4 Meanwhile, melt the remaining butter in a frying pan and fry the onions until tender and lightly browned. Add the mushrooms and fry until softened.

5 Add the mushrooms and onions to the casserole, cover and cook for a further 10 minutes or until the chicken is tender. Lift out the chicken and vegetables with a slotted spoon and put into a warmed serving dish. Cover and keep warm.

6 Bring the cooking liquid in the casserole to the boil. Whisk in the beurre manié, a piece at a time, until the sauce is shiny and syrupy. Check the seasoning.

7 Pour the sauce over the chicken. Serve with buttered noodles or rice.

Serves	A LITTLE EFFORT		NUTRITIONAL INFORMATION
4	**Preparation Time** 45 minutes	**Cooking Time** about 1 hour	**Per Serving** 787 calories, 51g fat (of which 22g saturates), 24g carbohydrate, 1.5g salt

Chicken Cacciatore

2 tbsp olive oil

8 boneless, skinless chicken thighs

2 garlic cloves, crushed

1 tsp dried thyme

1 tsp dried tarragon

150ml (¼ pint) white wine

400g can chopped tomatoes

12 pitted black olives

12 capers, rinsed and drained

ground black pepper

brown rice and broad beans or peas to serve

1 Heat the olive oil in a flameproof casserole over a high heat. Add the chicken and brown all over. Reduce the heat and add the garlic, thyme, tarragon and wine to the casserole. Stir for 1 minute, then add the tomatoes and season with pepper.

2 Bring to the boil, then reduce the heat, cover the casserole and simmer for 20 minutes or until the chicken is tender.

3 Lift the chicken out of the casserole and put to one side. Bubble the sauce for 5 minutes or until thickened, add the olives and capers, stir well and cook for a further 2–3 minutes.

4 Put the chicken into the sauce. Serve with brown rice and broad beans or peas.

Serves	EASY		NUTRITIONAL INFORMATION	
4	**Preparation Time** 5 minutes	**Cooking Time** 40 minutes	**Per Serving** 327 calories, 17g fat (of which 4g saturates), 3g carbohydrate, 1.3g salt	Gluten free Dairy free

2 tsp vegetable oil

1 green chilli, seeded and finely chopped (see page 23)

4cm (1½ in) piece fresh root ginger, peeled and finely grated

1 lemongrass stalk, cut into 3 pieces

225g (8oz) brown-cap or oyster mushrooms

1 tbsp Thai green curry paste

300ml (½ pint) coconut milk

150ml (¼ pint) chicken stock

1 tbsp Thai fish sauce

1 tsp light soy sauce

350g (12oz) skinless chicken breasts, cut into bite-size pieces

350g (12oz) cooked peeled large prawns

fresh coriander sprigs to garnish

Thai fragrant rice to serve

Thai Green Curry

1 Heat the oil in a wok or large frying pan, add the chilli, ginger, lemongrass and mushrooms and stir-fry for about 3 minutes or until the mushrooms begin to turn golden. Add the curry paste and fry for a further 1 minute.

2 Pour in the coconut milk, stock, fish sauce and soy sauce and bring to the boil. Stir in the chicken and simmer for about 8 minutes or until the chicken is cooked. Add the prawns and cook for a further 1 minute. Garnish with coriander sprigs and serve immediately with Thai fragrant rice.

EASY		NUTRITIONAL INFORMATION		Serves
Preparation Time 10 minutes	**Cooking Time** 15 minutes	**Per Serving** 132 calories, 2g fat (of which 0g saturates), 4g carbohydrate, 1.4g salt	Dairy free	6

Try Something Different

Omit the baby new potatoes and serve with mashed potatoes.

1 fresh rosemary sprig

2 bay leaves

1 small chicken, about 1.4kg (3lb)

1 red onion, cut into wedges

2 carrots, cut into chunks

2 leeks, trimmed and cut into chunks

2 celery sticks, cut into chunks

12 baby new potatoes

900ml (1½ pints) hot vegetable stock

200g (7oz) green beans, trimmed

salt and ground black pepper

Easy Chicken Casserole

1 Preheat the oven to 180°C (160°C fan oven) mark 4. Put the herbs and chicken into a large, flameproof casserole. Add the onion, carrots, leeks, celery, potatoes, stock and seasoning. Bring to the boil, then cook in the oven for 45 minutes or until the chicken is cooked through. To test the chicken, pierce the thickest part of the leg with a knife; the juices should run clear.

2 Add the beans and cook for 5 minutes. Remove the chicken and spoon the vegetables into six bowls. Carve the chicken and divide among the bowls, then ladle the cooking liquid over.

Serves	EASY		NUTRITIONAL INFORMATION	
6	**Preparation Time** 15 minutes	**Cooking Time** 50 minutes	**Per Serving** 323 calories, 18g fat (of which 5g saturates), 17g carbohydrate, 0.9g salt	Dairy free Gluten free

Chicken and Vegetable Hotpot

4 chicken breasts, with skin, about 125g (4oz) each
2 large parsnips, chopped
2 large carrots, chopped
300ml (½ pint) ready-made gravy
125g (4oz) cabbage, shredded
ground black pepper

1 Heat a non-stick frying pan or flameproof casserole until hot. Add the chicken breasts, skin side down, and cook for 5–6 minutes. Turn them over and add the parsnips and carrots. Cook for a further 7–8 minutes.

2 Pour the gravy over the chicken and vegetables, then cover and cook gently for 10 minutes.

3 Season with pepper and stir in the cabbage, then cover and continue to cook for 4–5 minutes until the chicken is cooked through, the cabbage has wilted and the vegetables are tender. Serve hot.

EASY		NUTRITIONAL INFORMATION		Serves
Preparation Time 5 minutes	**Cooking Time** 30 minutes	**Per Serving** 338 calories, 14g fat (of which 3g saturates), 14g carbohydrate, 1.2g salt	Dairy free	**4**

Chicken with Chorizo and Beans

1 tbsp olive oil

12 chicken pieces (6 drumsticks and 6 thighs)

175g (6oz) Spanish chorizo sausage, cubed

1 onion, finely chopped

2 large garlic cloves, crushed

1 tsp mild chilli powder

3 red peppers, seeded and roughly chopped

400g (14oz) passata

2 tbsp tomato purée

300ml (½ pint) chicken stock

2 x 400g cans butter beans, drained and rinsed

200g (7oz) baby new potatoes, halved

1 small bunch of thyme

1 bay leaf

200g (7oz) baby leaf spinach

1 Preheat the oven to 190°C (170°C fan oven) mark 5. Heat the olive oil in a large, flameproof casserole and brown the chicken pieces all over. Remove from the pan and set aside. Add the chorizo to the casserole and fry for 2–3 minutes until its oil starts to run.

2 Add the onion, garlic and chilli powder and fry over a low heat for 5 minutes or until soft.

3 Add the red peppers and cook for 2–3 minutes until soft. Stir in the passata, tomato purée, stock, beans, potatoes, thyme sprigs and bay leaf. Cover and simmer for 10 minutes.

4 Put the chicken and any juices back into the casserole. Bring to a simmer, then cover and cook in the oven for 30–35 minutes. If the sauce looks thin, put the casserole back on the hob over a medium heat and simmer to reduce until thickened.

5 Remove the thyme and bay leaf, and stir in the spinach until it wilts. Serve immediately.

Try Something Different

Use mixed beans instead of the butter beans.

EASY		NUTRITIONAL INFORMATION		Serves
Preparation Time 10 minutes	**Cooking Time** about 1 hour 10 minutes	**Per Serving** 690 calories, 41g fat (of which 12g saturates), 33g carbohydrate, 2.6g salt	Dairy free	**6**

Alsace Chicken

2 tbsp vegetable oil

8 chicken pieces (such as breasts, thighs and drumsticks)

125g (4oz) rindless smoked streaky bacon rashers, cut into strips

12 shallots, peeled but left whole

3 fresh tarragon sprigs

1 tbsp plain flour

150ml (¼ pint) Alsace Riesling white wine

500ml (18fl oz) hot chicken stock

3 tbsp crème fraîche

salt and ground black pepper

new potatoes (optional) and green vegetables to serve

1 Heat half the oil in a frying pan over a medium heat. Fry the chicken, in batches, until golden. Set aside.

2 Put the bacon into the same pan and fry gently to release its fat. Add the shallots and cook for 5 minutes, stirring occasionally, until both the shallots and bacon are lightly coloured.

3 Strip the leaves from the tarragon and set both the leaves and stalks aside. Sprinkle the flour over the shallots and bacon, and stir to absorb the juices. Cook for 1 minute, then gradually add the wine, stock and tarragon stalks. Put the chicken back into the pan, cover and simmer over a gentle heat for 45 minutes–1 hour until the chicken is cooked through.

4 Remove the chicken, bacon and shallots with a slotted spoon and keep warm. Discard the tarragon stalks. Bubble the sauce until reduced by half. Stir in the crème fraîche and tarragon leaves. Season with salt and pepper.

5 Turn off the heat, put the chicken, bacon and shallots back into the pan and stir to combine. Serve with new potatoes, if you like, and green vegetables.

Serves 4	EASY		NUTRITIONAL INFORMATION
	Preparation Time 20 minutes	**Cooking Time** 1 hour 20 minutes	**Per Serving** 484 calories, 24g fat (of which 8g saturates), 11g carbohydrate, 1.4g salt

2 tbsp vegetable oil

1 onion, finely sliced

2 garlic cloves, crushed

6 boneless, skinless chicken thighs, cut into strips

2 tbsp tikka masala curry paste

200g can chopped tomatoes

450ml (³/₄ pint) hot vegetable stock

225g (8oz) baby spinach leaves

fresh coriander leaves to garnish

rice, mango chutney and poppadoms to serve

Chicken Tikka Masala

1 Heat the oil in a large pan, add the onion and fry over a medium heat for 5–7 minutes until golden. Add the garlic and chicken and stir-fry for about 5 minutes or until golden.

2 Stir in the curry paste, then add the tomatoes and hot stock. Bring to the boil, then reduce the heat, cover the pan and simmer over a low heat for 15 minutes or until the chicken is cooked through.

3 Add the spinach to the curry, stir and cook until the leaves have just wilted. Garnish with coriander and serve with rice, mango chutney and poppadoms.

EASY		NUTRITIONAL INFORMATION		Serves
Preparation Time 15 minutes	**Cooking Time** 30 minutes	**Per Serving** 297 calories, 17g fat (of which 4g saturates), 4g carbohydrate, 0.6g salt	Dairy free	**4**

Cooking for Friends

Try Something Different

Pork and Apricot Burgers: replace the chicken with minced pork, use freshly chopped sage instead of tarragon, and add 100g (3½oz) chopped ready-to-eat dried apricots to the mixture before shaping.

Chicken Tarragon Burgers

225g (8oz) minced chicken

2 shallots, finely chopped

1 tbsp freshly chopped tarragon

25g (1oz) fresh breadcrumbs

1 large egg yolk

vegetable oil to grease

salt and ground black pepper

toasted burger buns, mayonnaise or Greek yogurt, salad leaves and tomato salad to serve

1 Put the chicken into a bowl with the shallots, tarragon, breadcrumbs and egg yolk. Mix well, then beat in about 75ml (2½fl oz) cold water and season with salt and pepper.

2 Lightly oil a foil-lined baking sheet. Divide the chicken mixture into four portions and put on the foil. Using the back of a wet spoon, flatten each portion to a thickness of 2.5cm (1in). Cover and chill for 30 minutes.

3 Preheat the barbecue or grill. If cooking on the barbecue lift the burgers straight on to the grill rack; if cooking under the grill slide the baking sheet under the grill. Cook the burgers for 5–6 minutes on each side until cooked through, then serve in a toasted burger bun with a dollop of mayonnaise or Greek yogurt, a few salad leaves and tomato salad.

Serves 2	EASY		NUTRITIONAL INFORMATION	
	Preparation Time 30 minutes, plus 30 minutes chilling	**Cooking Time** 12 minutes	**Per Serving** 205 calories, 4g fat (of which 1g saturates), 12g carbohydrate, 0.4g salt	Dairy free

10 skinless chicken pieces, scored with a knife

1 tbsp each ground coriander and paprika

2 tsp ground cumin

a pinch of freshly grated nutmeg

1 fresh Scotch bonnet or other hot red chilli, seeded and chopped (see page 23)

1 onion, chopped

5 fresh thyme sprigs, leaves stripped, plus extra to garnish

4 garlic cloves, crushed

2 tbsp dark soy sauce

juice of 1 lemon

2 tbsp vegetable oil

2 tbsp light muscovado sugar

350g (12oz) American easy-cook rice

25g (1oz) butter

2 x 300g cans black-eyed beans, drained and rinsed

salt and ground black pepper

Caribbean Chicken

1 Put the chicken into a bowl and sprinkle with ¹/₂ tsp salt, some pepper, the coriander, paprika, cumin and nutmeg. Add the chilli, onion, thyme leaves and garlic, then pour the soy sauce and lemon juice over and stir to combine. Cover and chill for at least 4 hours.

2 Heat a 3.4 litre (6 pint) heavy-based pan over medium heat for 2 minutes. Add the oil and sugar and cook for 3 minutes to a rich caramel colour – don't let it burn. Remove the chicken from the marinade and add to the caramel mixture, cover and cook over a medium heat for 5 minutes. Turn the chicken and cook, covered, for 5 minutes or until evenly browned. Add the onion, chilli and any juices from the marinade. Turn again, then cover and cook for 10 minutes. Stir in the rice and add 900ml (1¹/₂ pints) water. Add the butter and ¹/₂ tsp salt. Cover and simmer for 20 minutes or until the rice is tender and most of the liquid has been absorbed. Mix in the beans, cover and cook for 3–5 minutes until the liquid has been absorbed, taking care that the rice doesn't stick to the bottom of the pan. Garnish with thyme and serve hot.

EASY		NUTRITIONAL INFORMATION	Serves
Preparation Time 40 minutes, plus at least 4 hours marinating	**Cooking Time** 45–50 minutes	**Per Serving** 617 calories, 39g fat (of which 12g saturates), 25g carbohydrate, 2.1g salt	**5**

Easy Chicken and Ham Pie

4 ready-roasted chicken breasts, about 125g (4oz) each, shredded

100g (3¹/₂oz) cooked smoked ham, cubed

150ml (¹/₄ pint) double cream

75ml (2¹/₂fl oz) chicken gravy

2 tbsp finely chopped tarragon

1 tsp cornflour

¹/₂ tsp ready-made English mustard

250g (9oz) ready-rolled puff pastry

1 medium egg, beaten

ground black pepper

seasonal vegetables to serve

1 Preheat the oven to 200°C (180°C fan oven) mark 6. Put the chicken into a large bowl with the ham, cream, gravy, tarragon, cornflour and mustard. Season with pepper and mix well.

2 Spoon into a shallow 1 litre (1³/₄ pint) baking dish. Unroll the puff pastry and position over the top of the dish to cover. Trim to fit the dish, then press the edges down lightly around the rim. Brush the egg over the pastry. Cook for 30–35 minutes until the pastry is golden and puffed up. Serve hot, with vegetables.

Try Something Different

Replace the chicken with 450g (1lb) cooked turkey and replace the tarragon with chopped thyme leaves.

EASY		NUTRITIONAL INFORMATION	Serves
Preparation Time 15 minutes	**Cooking Time** 30–35 minutes	**Per Serving** 402 calories, 28g fat (of which 9g saturates), 17g carbohydrate, 1.2g salt	**6**

Chicken Tagine with Apricots and Almonds

2 tbsp olive oil

4 chicken thighs

1 onion, chopped

2 tsp ground cinnamon

2 tbsp clear honey

150g (5oz) ready-to-eat dried apricots

75g (3oz) blanched almonds

250ml (9fl oz) hot chicken stock

salt and ground black pepper

flaked almonds to garnish

couscous to serve (see page 27)

1 Heat 1 tbsp olive oil in a large, flameproof casserole over a medium heat. Add the chicken and fry for 5 minutes or until brown. Remove from the casserole and put to one side to keep warm.

2 Add the onion to the casserole with the remaining oil and fry for 10 minutes or until softened.

3 Put the chicken back into the casserole with the cinnamon, honey, apricots, almonds and stock. Season well with salt and pepper, stir once, then cover and bring to the boil. Simmer for 45 minutes or until the chicken is falling off the bone.

4 Garnish with the flaked almonds and serve hot with couscous.

Serves 4	EASY		NUTRITIONAL INFORMATION	
	Preparation Time 10 minutes	**Cooking Time** about 1 hour	**Per Serving** 376 calories, 22g fat (of which 4g saturates), 19g carbohydrate, 0.5g salt	Dairy free

Chicken Kebabs with Tabbouleh

1 tbsp balsamic vinegar

3 tbsp olive oil

grated zest and juice of 1 lime

1 garlic clove, crushed

4 large skinless chicken breasts, about 700g (1½ lb) total weight, cut into 2.5cm (1in) cubes

For the tabbouleh

75g (3oz) bulgur wheat

½ cucumber, halved lengthways, deseeded and diced

4 plum tomatoes, deseeded and diced

1 small red onion, finely chopped

4 tbsp each freshly chopped mint and flat-leafed parsley

3 tbsp olive oil

juice of 1 lime

1 garlic clove, crushed

ground black pepper

lime wedges and fresh mint sprigs to garnish

1 In a large bowl, whisk together the balsamic vinegar, olive oil, lime zest and juice, and 1 garlic clove. Add the chicken, mix well, then cover and chill for at least 2 hours, preferably overnight.

2 To make the tabbouleh, put the bulgur wheat into a bowl, cover with double its volume of boiling water and leave to soak for 15 minutes. Drain the bulgur wheat, squeeze out the liquid and put back into the bowl. Stir in the cucumber, tomatoes, onion and herbs. Season with pepper. Whisk together the olive oil, lime juice and garlic in a small bowl. Add to the bulgur wheat and mix gently but thoroughly until the bulgur is well coated. Cover and chill.

3 Preheat the barbecue, grill or griddle. Soak eight wooden skewers in water for 20 minutes. Remove the chicken from the marinade, thread on to the skewers and cook for 10–12 minutes, turning every now and then, until cooked through. Serve with the tabbouleh. Garnish with lime wedges and mint sprigs.

EASY		NUTRITIONAL INFORMATION		Serves
Preparation Time 35 minutes, plus at least 2 hours marinating	**Cooking Time** 10–12 minutes, plus soaking	**Per Serving** 330 calories, 8g fat (of which 1g saturates), 19g carbohydrate, 0.3g salt	Dairy free	**4**

Simple Paella

1 litre (1³/₄ pints) chicken stock
¹/₂ tsp saffron
6 boneless, skinless chicken thighs
5 tbsp extra virgin olive oil
1 large onion, chopped
4 large garlic cloves, crushed
1 tsp paprika
2 red peppers, seeded and sliced
400g can chopped tomatoes
350g (12oz) long-grain rice
200ml (7fl oz) dry sherry
500g (1lb 2oz) cooked mussels
200g (7oz) cooked tiger prawns
juice of ¹/₂ lemon
salt and ground black pepper
lemon wedges and fresh flat-leafed parsley to serve

1 Heat the stock, then add the saffron and leave to infuse for 30 minutes. Meanwhile, cut each chicken thigh into three pieces.

2 Heat half the olive oil in a large frying pan and, working in batches, fry the chicken for 3–5 minutes until pale golden brown. Set the chicken aside.

3 Lower the heat slightly and add the remaining oil. Fry the onion for 5 minutes or until soft. Add the garlic and paprika and stir for 1 minute. Add the chicken, red peppers and tomatoes.

4 Stir in the rice, then add one-third of the stock and bring to the boil. Season with salt and pepper.

5 Reduce the heat to a simmer. Cook, uncovered, stirring continuously, until most of the liquid is absorbed.

6 Add the remaining stock a little at a time, letting it become absorbed into the rice before adding more. (This should take about 25 minutes.) Add the sherry and continue cooking for another 2 minutes – the rice should be quite wet, as it will continue to absorb liquid.

7 Add the mussels and prawns to the pan, including all their juices, with the lemon juice. Stir them in and cook for 5 minutes to heat through. Adjust the seasoning and garnish with lemon wedges and fresh parsley.

Serves	A LITTLE EFFORT		NUTRITIONAL INFORMATION
6	**Preparation Time** 15 minutes, plus infusing	**Cooking Time** 50 minutes	**Per Serving** 554 calories, 16g fat (of which 3g saturates), 58g carbohydrate, 0.5g salt

Try Something Different

Instead of chicken, try this recipe with sausages; roast them for 20–30 minutes.

Italian marinade: mix 1 crushed garlic clove with 4 tbsp olive oil, the juice of 1 lemon and 1 tsp dried oregano. If you like, leave to marinate for 1–2 hours before cooking.

Oriental marinade: mix together 2 tbsp soy sauce, 1 tsp demerara sugar, 2 tbsp dry sherry or apple juice, 1 tsp finely chopped fresh root ginger and 1 crushed garlic clove.

Honey and mustard marinade: mix together 2 tbsp grain mustard, 3 tbsp clear honey and the grated zest and juice of 1 lemon.

Sticky Chicken Thighs

1 garlic clove, crushed

1 tbsp clear honey

1 tbsp Thai sweet chilli sauce

4 chicken thighs

rice and green salad to serve

1 Preheat the oven to 200°C (180°C fan oven) mark 6. Put the garlic into a bowl with the honey and chilli sauce, and mix together. Add the chicken thighs and toss to coat.

2 Put into a roasting tin and roast for 15–20 minutes until the chicken is golden and cooked through. Serve with rice and a crisp green salad.

Serves	EASY		NUTRITIONAL INFORMATION	
4	**Preparation Time** 5 minutes	**Cooking Time** 20 minutes	**Per Serving** 218 calories, 12g fat (of which 3g saturates), 5g carbohydrate, 0.4g salt	Gluten free Dairy free

Cook's Tip

White sauce: to make 600ml (1 pint) white sauce, melt 25g (1oz) butter in a pan, then stir in 25g (1oz) plain flour. Cook, stirring constantly, for 1 minute. Remove from the heat and gradually pour in 600ml (1 pint) milk, beating after each addition. Return to the heat and cook, stirring, until the sauce has thickened and is velvety and smooth. Season with salt, black pepper and freshly grated nutmeg.

Oven-baked Chicken with Garlic Potatoes

2 medium baking potatoes, thinly sliced

a little freshly grated nutmeg

600ml (1 pint) white sauce (use a ready-made sauce or make your own, see Cook's Tip)

$\frac{1}{2}$ x 390g can fried onions

250g (9oz) frozen peas

450g (1lb) cooked chicken, shredded

20g pack garlic butter, sliced

a little butter to grease

salt and ground black pepper

steamed vegetables and Granary bread (optional) to serve

1 Preheat the oven to 180°C (160°C fan oven) mark 4. Layer half the potatoes over the base of a 2.4 litre (4$\frac{1}{4}$ pint) shallow ovenproof dish and season with the nutmeg, salt and pepper. Pour the white sauce over and shake the dish, so that the sauce settles through the gaps in the potatoes.

2 Spread half the onions on top, then scatter over half the peas. Arrange the shredded chicken on top, then add the remaining peas and onions. Finish with the remaining potato, arranged in an even layer, and dot with garlic butter. Season with salt and pepper.

3 Cover tightly with buttered foil and cook for 1 hour. Turn the heat up to 200°C (180°C fan oven) mark 6, remove the foil and continue to cook for 20–30 minutes until the potatoes are golden and tender. Serve with steamed vegetables and, if you like, some Granary bread to mop up the juices.

EASY		NUTRITIONAL INFORMATION	Serves
Preparation Time 10 minutes	**Cooking Time** 1½ hours	**Per Serving** 376 calories, 16g fat (of which 5g saturates), 32g carbohydrate, 1.2g salt	**6**

Perfect Roast Chicken

1 chicken, about 1.8kg (4lb)

25g (1oz) butter, softened

2 tbsp olive oil

1½ lemons, cut in half

1 small head of garlic, cut in half horizontally

salt and ground black pepper

potatoes and seasonal vegetables to serve

1 Preheat the oven to 220°C (200°C fan oven) mark 7. Put the chicken into a roasting tin just large enough to hold it comfortably. Spread the butter all over the chicken, then drizzle with the olive oil and season with salt and pepper.

2 Squeeze lemon juice over it, then put one lemon half inside the chicken. Put the other halves and the garlic into the roasting tin.

3 Put the chicken into the oven for 15 minutes, then turn the heat down to 190°C (170°C fan oven) mark 5 and cook for a further 45 minutes–1 hour until the leg juices run clear when pierced with a skewer or sharp knife. While the bird is cooking, baste from time to time with the pan juices. Add a splash of water to the tin if the juices dry out.

4 Take the chicken out, put on to a warm plate and cover with foil. Leave for 15 minutes before carving, so that the juices that have risen to the surface can soak back into the meat. This will make it more moist and easier to slice. Mash some of the garlic into the pan juices and serve the gravy with the chicken. Serve with potatoes and seasonal vegetables.

EASY		NUTRITIONAL INFORMATION	Serves
Preparation Time 5 minutes	**Cooking Time** 1 hour–1¼ hours, plus resting	**Per Serving** 639 calories, 46g fat (of which 13g saturates), 0g carbohydrate, 0.6g salt	**4**

Get Ahead

Complete the recipe to the end of step 4. Cool quickly, then freeze in an airtight container for up to one month.
To use Thaw overnight at cool room temperature. Preheat the oven to 220°C (200°C fan oven) mark 7. Put the chicken back into the casserole and reheat in the oven for 15 minutes. Reduce the oven temperature to 180°C (160°C fan oven) mark 4 and cook for a further 25 minutes.

Slow-braised Garlic Chicken

2 tbsp olive oil

1 tbsp freshly chopped thyme

125g (4oz) chestnut mushrooms, finely chopped

6 whole chicken legs (drumsticks and thighs)

18 thin slices pancetta

2 tbsp plain flour

25g (1oz) butter

18 small shallots

12 garlic cloves, unpeeled but split

750ml bottle full-bodied white wine, such as Chardonnay

2 bay leaves

salt and ground black pepper

1 Preheat the oven to 180°C (160°C fan oven) mark 4. Heat 1 tbsp oil in a frying pan and fry the thyme and mushrooms until all the moisture has evaporated and the mixture is quite dry. Season and leave to cool.

2 Loosen the skin away from one chicken leg and spoon a little of the mushroom paste underneath. Season the leg all over with salt and pepper, then wrap three pancetta slices around the thigh end. Repeat with the remaining chicken legs, then dust using 1 tbsp flour.

3 Melt the butter in a frying pan with the remaining oil over a high heat. Fry the chicken legs, in batches of two, seam side down, until golden. Turn the legs, brown the other side, then transfer to a deep casserole. The browning process should take about 8–10 minutes per batch.

4 Put the shallots and garlic into the frying pan and cook for 10 minutes or until browned. Sprinkle over the remaining flour and cook for 1 minute. Pour in the wine and bring to the boil, stirring. Pour into the casserole with the chicken and add the bay leaves. Cover and cook in the oven for 1½ hours. Serve hot.

Serves 6	A LITTLE EFFORT		NUTRITIONAL INFORMATION
	Preparation Time 30 minutes	**Cooking Time** about 2 hours	**Per Serving** 506 calories, 28g fat (of which 9g saturates), 10g carbohydrate, 1g salt

2 tbsp olive oil

300g (11oz) boneless, skinless chicken thighs, cut into chunks

75g (3oz) French sausage, chopped

2 celery sticks, chopped

1 large onion, finely chopped

225g (8oz) long-grain rice

1 tbsp tomato purée

2 tsp Cajun seasoning

500ml (18fl oz) hot chicken stock

1 bay leaf

4 large tomatoes, roughly chopped

200g (7oz) raw tiger prawns

Jambalaya

1 Heat 1 tbsp olive oil in a large pan and fry the chicken and sausage over a medium heat until browned. Remove with a slotted spoon and set aside.

2 Add the remaining oil to the pan with the celery and onion. Fry gently for 15 minutes or until the vegetables are softened but not coloured. Tip in the rice and stir for 1 minute to coat in the oil. Add the tomato purée and Cajun seasoning, and cook for another 2 minutes.

3 Pour in the hot stock and put the browned chicken and sausage back into the pan with the bay leaf and tomatoes. Simmer for about 20–25 minutes until the stock is fully absorbed and the rice is cooked.

4 Stir in the prawns and cover the pan. Turn off the heat and leave to stand for 10 minutes or until the prawns have turned pink. Serve immediately.

EASY		NUTRITIONAL INFORMATION		Serves
Preparation Time 15 minutes	**Cooking Time** about 1 hour	**Per Serving** 567 calories, 27g fat (of which 8g saturates), 38g carbohydrate, 1.1g salt	Dairy free	**4**

Coronation Chicken

1 tbsp vegetable oil

1 onion, chopped

1 tbsp ground coriander

1 tbsp ground cumin

1½ tsp ground turmeric

1½ tsp paprika

150ml (¼ pint) dry white wine

500ml (18fl oz) chicken stock

6 boneless, skinless chicken breasts or thighs

2 bay leaves

2 fresh thyme sprigs

2 fresh parsley sprigs

salt and ground black pepper

3–4 tbsp freshly chopped flat-leafed parsley to garnish

mixed leaf salad and French bread to serve

For the dressing

150ml (¼ pint) mayonnaise

5 tbsp natural yogurt

2 tbsp mango chutney

125g (4oz) ready-to-eat dried apricots, chopped

juice of ½ lemon

1 Heat the oil in a large, heavy-based pan, add the onion and fry for 5–10 minutes until softened and golden. Add the spices and cook, stirring, for 1–2 minutes.

2 Pour in the wine, bring to the boil and let it bubble for 5 minutes to reduce right down. Add the stock and bring to the boil again.

3 Season the chicken with salt and pepper, then add to the pan with the bay leaves and herb sprigs. Cover and bring to the boil. Reduce the heat to low and poach the chicken for 25 minutes or until cooked through. Cool quickly by plunging the base of the pan into a sink of cold water, replacing the water as it warms up.

4 Meanwhile, to make the dressing, mix the mayonnaise, yogurt and mango chutney together in a bowl. Drain the cooled stock from the chicken and whisk 200ml (7fl oz) into the mayonnaise mixture. Add the apricots and lemon juice, and season well.

5 Stir the chicken into the curried mayonnaise, then cover and chill until required. Scatter with chopped parsley and serve with a mixed leaf salad and French bread.

Serves	EASY		NUTRITIONAL INFORMATION
6	**Preparation Time** 20 minutes	**Cooking Time** about 50 minutes	**Per Serving** 425 calories, 26g fat (of which 4g saturates), 14g carbohydrate, 0.6g salt

Garlic and Thyme Chicken

2 garlic cloves, crushed

2 tbsp freshly chopped thyme leaves

2 tbsp olive oil

4 chicken thighs

salt and ground black pepper

1 Preheat the barbecue or grill. Mix together the garlic, thyme and olive oil in a large bowl. Season with salt and pepper.

2 Using a sharp knife, make two or three slits in each chicken thigh. Put the chicken into the bowl and toss to coat thoroughly. Barbecue or grill for 5–7 minutes on each side until golden and cooked through.

Serves 4	EASY		NUTRITIONAL INFORMATION	
	Preparation Time 10 minutes	**Cooking Time** 10–15 minutes	**Per Serving** 135 calories, 6g fat (of which 1g saturates), trace carbohydrate, 0.2g salt	Gluten free Dairy free

Cook's Tip

Sage has a naturally strong, pungent taste, so you need only a little to flavour the chicken. Don't be tempted to add more than just one leaf to each chicken breast or it will overpower the finished dish.

Stuffed Chicken Breasts

vegetable oil to grease
150g (5oz) ball mozzarella
4 skinless chicken breasts, about 125g (4oz) each
4 sage leaves
8 slices Parma ham
new potatoes and spinach to serve

1 Preheat the oven to 200°C (180°C fan oven) mark 6. Lightly grease a baking sheet. Slice the mozzarella into eight, then put two slices on to each chicken piece. Top each with a sage leaf.

2 Wrap each piece of chicken in two slices of Parma ham, covering the mozzarella.

3 Put on to the prepared baking sheet and cook in the oven for 20 minutes or until the chicken is cooked through. Serve with new potatoes and spinach.

EASY		NUTRITIONAL INFORMATION		Serves
Preparation Time 5 minutes	**Cooking Time** 20 minutes	**Per Serving** 297 calories, 13g fat (of which 7g saturates), trace carbohydrate, 1.4g salt	Gluten free	**4**

Chicken and Leek Filo Pie

75g (3oz) unsalted butter

2 large leeks, trimmed and finely sliced

2 large carrots, finely chopped

1 tbsp plain flour

400ml (14fl oz) hot chicken stock

2 tsp Dijon mustard

3 tbsp double cream

350g (12oz) cooked chicken (leftovers are fine), cut into chunks

2 tbsp freshly chopped parsley

12 sheets filo pastry, thawed if frozen

salt and ground black pepper

green salad to serve

1 Preheat the oven to 200°C (180°C fan oven) mark 6. Melt 25g (1oz) butter in a pan over a low heat. Cook the leeks and carrots for 15 minutes or until softened but not coloured. Stir in the flour and cook for 1 minute. Gradually add the stock, stirring constantly, until the sauce is smooth. Simmer for 10 minutes.

2 Stir in the mustard and cream, and season with salt and pepper. Add the cooked chicken and parsley and tip into a 1.7 litre (3 pint) ovenproof dish.

3 Melt the remaining butter in a small pan. Unroll the filo pastry and cover with a clean, damp teatowel. Put a single sheet on a board and brush with a little of the butter. Roughly scrunch up the pastry and put on top of the chicken mixture. Continue with the remaining filo until the top of the pie is covered.

4 Cook for 20–25 minutes until the filo is golden and the chicken mixture is bubbling. Serve with green salad.

Get Ahead

Complete the recipe up to the end of step 2, but allow the sauce to cool completely before adding the chicken. Chill for up to two days or freeze for up to one month.
To use If frozen, thaw overnight at cool room temperature, then complete the recipe.

EASY		NUTRITIONAL INFORMATION	Serves
Preparation Time 15 minutes	**Cooking Time** about 50 minutes	**Per Serving** 331 calories, 18g fat (of which 10g saturates), 27g carbohydrate, 0.4g salt	**6**

Index

COOKING MEASURES

TEMPERATURE

°C	Fan oven	Gas mark	°C	Fan oven	Gas mark
110	90	¼	190	170	5
130	110	½	200	180	6
140	120	1	220	200	7
150	130	2	230	210	8
170	150	3	240	220	9
180	160	4			

LIQUIDS

Metric	Imperial	Metric	Imperial
5ml	1 tsp	200ml	7fl oz
15ml	1 tbsp	250ml	9fl oz
25ml	1fl oz	300ml	½ pint
50ml	2fl oz	500ml	18fl oz
100ml	3½fl oz	600ml	1 pint
125ml	4fl oz	900ml	1½ pints
150ml	5fl oz / ¼ pint	1 litre	1¾ pints
175ml	6fl oz		

MEASURES

Metric	Imperial	Metric	Imperial
5mm	¼in	10cm	4in
1cm	½in	15cm	6in
2cm	¾in	18cm	7in
2.5cm	1in	20.5cm	8in
3cm	1¼in	23cm	9in
4cm	1½in	25.5cm	10in
5cm	2in	28cm	11in
7.5cm	3in	30.5cm	12in

WEIGHTS

Metric	Imperial	Metric	Imperial
15g	½oz	275g	10oz
25g	1oz	300g	11oz
40g	1½oz	350g	12oz
50g	2oz	375g	13oz
75g	3oz	400g	14oz
100g	3½oz	425g	15oz
125g	4oz	450g	1lb
150g	5oz	550g	1¼lb
175g	6oz	700g	1½lb
200g	7oz	900g	2lb
225g	8oz	1.1kg	2½lb
250g	9oz		

Always remember...

- Ovens and grills must be preheated to the specified temperature.
- For fan ovens the temperature should be set to 20°C less.
- Use one set of measurements; do not mix metric and imperial.
- All spoon measures are level.

NOTES

- Both metric and imperial measures are given for the recipes. Follow either set of measures, not a mixture of both, as they are not interchangeable.
- All spoon measures are level. 1 tsp = 5ml spoon; 1 tbsp = 15ml spoon.
- Ovens and grills must be preheated to the specified temperature.
- Use sea salt and freshly ground black pepper unless otherwise suggested.
- Fresh herbs should be used unless dried herbs are specified in a recipe.
- Medium eggs should be used except where otherwise specified. Free-range eggs are recommended.
- Note that certain recipes, including mayonnaise, lemon curd and some cold desserts, contain raw or lightly cooked eggs. The young, elderly, pregnant women and anyone with an immune-deficiency disease should avoid these, because of the slight risk of salmonella.
- Calorie, fat and carbohydrate counts per serving are provided for the recipes.
- If you are following a gluten- or dairy-free diet, check the labels on all pre-packaged food goods.
- Nutritional information for serving suggestions do not take gluten- or dairy-free diets into account.

Picture credits
Photographers: Neil Barclay (pages 2, 32, 34, 37, 39, 40, 41, 49, 56, 60, 63, 75, 80, 83, 85, 95, 96, 102, 103, 113, 118, 119, 121, 124, 127); Nicki Dowey (pages 6, 33, 36, 47, 48, 52, 54, 55, 58, 59, 61, 71, 7, 72, 78, 90, 92, 98, 100, 106, 111, 114, 122, 123); Craig Robertson (pages 8–29, 42, 66, 70, 79, 82, 91, 93, 99, 107, 108, 110); Lucinda Symons (pages 18, 28, 73, 115, 116); Will Heap (pages 50, 76); Martin Brigdale (pages 53, 67, 68, 77, 84, 97); Clive Streeter (page 88)